THE OTTOMAN EMPIRE:
Its Record and Legacy

WAYNE S. VUCINICH

Professor of History
Stanford University

THE ANVIL SERIES
under the general editorship of
LOUIS L. SNYDER

ROBERT E. KRIEGER PUBLISHING COMPANY
HUNTINGTON, NEW YORK

Original Edition 1965
Reprint Edition 1979

Printed and Published by
ROBERT E. KRIEGER PUBLISHING COMPANY, INC.
645 NEW YORK AVENUE
HUNTINGTON, NEW YORK 11743

Copyright © 1965 by
Wayne S. Vucinich
Reprinted by Arrangement with
D. VAN NOSTRAND COMPANY, INC.

Printed in the United States of America

Library of Congress Cataloging in Publication Data

Vucinich, Wayne S.
    The Ottoman Empire, its Record and Legacy.

    Reprint of the edition published by Van Nostrand, Princeton, N. J., in series: An Anvil original.
    Bibliography: p.
    Includes index.
    1. Turkey—History—Ottoman Empire, 1288-1918.
        I. Title
[DR486-V82 1979]   949.6   78.11514
ISBN 0-88275-785-7

National Series Data Program
ISSN #0570-1062

PREFACE

The Ottoman Empire was an intricate network of social systems and subsystems, which changed from one period to another far more than is generally believed. The vast array of constituent elements shifted in relation to each other much like the particles in a kaleidoscope. Not only did they differ, but they often displayed important variations within themselves.

The Ottoman Empire was enfeebled by its own deliberate policy of isolating from each other the several distinct component cultures. It failed to instill in its diverse subjects a sense of belonging. After the sixteenth century the inherent weaknesses of the Ottoman state stood forth fully revealed, and the Empire entered a period of ineluctable decline. In the following pages an attempt will be made to give a concise picture of the Ottoman Empire in the time of its flowering and in the time of its decay, with brief comments on its many-sided legacy.

In the preparation of this modest compendium the author has relied on the works listed in the bibliography, including such masterly studies of Ottoman civilization as H. A. R. Gibb and Harold Bowen, *Islamic Society and the West;* Bernard Lewis, *The Emergence of Modern Turkey;* and many other well-known works.

In dealing with the vexatious problem of transliteration, I have decided to use names and terms commonly known in the West in their generally accepted English forms and to give others in a slightly modified version of the modern Turkish alphabet. This modification consists of the following:

> *j* (as in *joke*) in place of *c*
> *ch* (as in *church*) in place of *ç*
> *gh* (a guttural *gh* or hard *g*) in place of *ğ*
> *kh* (a scraped guttural *h*) in place of *h*
> *i* (as in *bird*) in place of *ı*
> *sh* (as in *shirt*) in place of *ş*

3

The Modern Turkish *ö* (as *eu* in French *peu*) and *ü* (as *u* in French *tu*) were not transliterated. Some words, especially the religious and legal terms, are given in the Arabic form rather than the Turkish.

A number of persons have given me of their time and knowledge. I am particularly indebted to three colleagues who read the manuscript and made valuable suggestions for its improvements: Dr. George S. Rentz, Curator of the Middle East Collection, Hoover Institution, and Lecturer in the Department of History, Stanford University; Professor Stanford J. Shaw of the Center for Middle Eastern Studies, Harvard University; and Dr. Ernest E. Ramsaur, Jr., of the Department of State, Washington, D.C. I am also grateful to several of my students who lent me a helping hand in various ways.

W.S.V

TABLE OF CONTENTS

Part I

THE OTTOMAN EMPIRE

— 1 —

THE ORIGIN OF THE OTTOMAN STATE

The origin of the Ottoman state has long been a subject of historical controversy. Older historians such as Hammer-Purgstall, Zinkeisen, and Iorga more or less accepted the traditional explanation based on the Turkish chronicles. It has since been established that while some of the early chronicles are "substantially correct," others are replete with legends and myths. The later chronicles were apparently composed to enhance the prestige of the Ottoman ruling house with a long line of distinguished ancestors. This tradition traces the Ottomans to a Central Asian ancestral home, to the nomadic tribe of the Kayi Turks, a branch of the Oghuz, who emigrated to Anatolia under the pressure of the Mongol invasion in the thirteenth century.

By a critical assessment of philological and epigraphical data, Wittek discloses glaring contradictions in the traditional genealogy and demonstrates that the Kayi lineage of the Ottoman rulers is fictitious. Wittek shows convincingly that the Ottomans did not come to Anatolia "as a new wave of invasion" in the thirteenth century. He further proves that the Ottomans in fact did not consider themselves a distinct tribal entity or a new "race," but merely a "community of ghazis" (frontier warriors for the faith). The contention advanced by Gibbons that the Ottoman leaders were "self-made men" who adopted Islam after they arrived in Western Anatolia, and that they were fused with the indigenous Greeks

9

to produce the Ottoman nation, is rejected by most responsible historians. A Turkish historian, Mehmed Fuad Köprülü, identifies the Ottomans as only one of many closely related Turkish groups which invaded Anatolia; the term "Ottoman," he explains, is a "political" and not an "ethnic" concept.

Many uncertainties still shroud the history of the Ottomans before the thirteenth century. Historians accept as a fact that the founder of the Ottoman state was Osman (Othman), son of Ertoghrul. The father had received from the Seljuk sultan Ala al-Din II a landed fief (beylik or emirate) based on the city of Sögüt on the Byzantine border in northwestern Anatolia. With a certain number of Turkoman tribesmen Ertoghrul guarded the frontier, and like other warriors led incursions into Byzantine territory. His son Osman inherited the fief and established the dynasty that bore his name—Osmanli, or Ottoman.

What Accounts for Ottoman Successes? One paramount question still asked by historians is how a small band of nomadic and semi-nomadic Turks could come to rule an organized state in which there were large numbers of non-Muslims. Of great importance was the frontier position of the territory granted Ertoghrul, the scene of almost constant warfare between the Muslim *ghazis* and the Christian *akritoi* (frontier defenders). The opportunity to struggle for the faith attracted *ghazis* from many parts of the Islamic world, and particularly Turkomans then fleeing into Anatolia before the Mongols. The *ghazi* organization supplied the basis for the political structure of an emirate.

The long period of Christian-Muslim coexistence and mutual influence suggests that the early Ottomans were not so primitive as is sometimes believed and that they indeed had adequate resources for building a state. The Seljuk legacy of urban life and intellectual activity contributed greatly to the growth of the new state. The institutions of the *akhis* (brotherhood of merchants and artisans) and the *ulema* (a class of teachers and interpreters of Islam) provided the foundations for the Ottoman administrative system.

The growth and expansion of the Ottoman state were also facilitated by the Muslim system of guilds (*esnaf*), and by the strong discipline of the leaders of associations of youth, whose members were bound together by the strict moral and ethical ideas of the *futuwwa,* the *ghazi* code of honor. The chance of winning booty attracted many to the Ottoman forces. The ability of the early rulers also played a part in the initial Ottoman successes. Finally, the political decline of Byzantium and feudal anarchy in the Balkans contributed to the relative ease with which the Ottomans expanded.

Few peoples have been so intransigently Muslim as the Ottomans, who took the missionary aspect of Islam seriously. Non-Muslims submitting to them were assigned to a special sphere in which they recognized the supremacy of Islam and paid tribute. Many Christians voluntarily adopted Islam to win positions in the Ottoman system.

The Roots of Ottoman Civilization.   What kind of a civilization did the Ottomans develop? Should the Ottoman Empire be regarded as merely an extension of the Seljuk and Byzantine states or as a distinct polity? Ottoman civilization had its roots in local Anatolian, Muslim, and Turkish civilizations, but in time it absorbed elements of other cultures. Indigenous Anatolian influences —Hittite, Armenian, Greek, and others—on the Turks are acknowledged by most historians. Byzantine influence was intensified after the conquest of Istanbul, though Nicolae Iorga, who referred to Istanbul as the Turanian (Turkish) Rome, and certain other writers exaggerate its importance.

Islam was the basic element of Ottoman society. First exposed to it along the borders of the Caliphate in Central Asia, the Turks from then on emphasized the application of its militant doctrines to life on the frontier. The influence of Central Asia on Ottoman society, overshadowed for a time by Islam, revived in the fourteenth century when the Ottomans absorbed large numbers of Turkish nomads in Anatolia. The nomads aroused an awareness in the Ottomans of their Turkish origin; the Ottoman Sultans assumed the old Turkish title of *khan* and adopted the Oghuz legend to explain the origin of their dynasty. Apart from this, however, the Ottomans put little emphasis on Turkish nationality until the nineteenth century.

— 2 —

BUILDING AN EMPIRE

The Ottoman state and dynasty, which were founded by Osman (1299-1326) and bore his name, survived until after the First World War. A long time was required, however, for the Ottoman state to grow into an empire. Orkhan (1326-1359) greatly strengthened the administrative system and the military organization of the young state and conquered new territories at the expense of both Muslims and Greeks. Like his predecessors, he called himself "Sultan, son of the Sultan of the Ghazis, Ghazi, son of the Ghazi . . . marchlord of the horizons, hero of the world." Orkhan seized Brusa (Bursa) and Nicomedia (Izmit) from the Byzantine Empire and made the former the Ottoman capital. In 1331 the Ottomans took Nicaea (Iznik), virtually ending Byzantine rule in Asia Minor. The first important pillaging forays in the Balkans occurred in the second quarter of the fourteenth century.

The Invasion of the Balkans. The Ottomans initially directed their principal expansionist drive against the Byzantine state, which was in the throes of a dire internal crisis. Playing Greek leaders off against each other, they established a foothold on the Gallipoli peninsula, the European side of the Dardanelles, in 1354. By the time of Murad I (1359-1389) an excellent military organization and the mobility of its light cavalry gave the Ottomans superiority over their Christian adversaries. Political anarchy in the Balkans, caused by feudal strife and internecine wars among the rulers, aggravated by Hungarian and Venetian intrigues, aided the Ottoman military advance. In 1362 Murad I captured Adrian-

ople (Edirne), which he made his new capital, and nine
years later he won a major victory on the Maritsa River.
Far more decisive was the Ottoman victory over the
Serbs and their allies at Kosovo ("The Field of the
Blackbirds") in 1389, giving the Turks the key to the
whole Balkan Peninsula. Both the Sultan and the Serbian
King Lazar perished in the battle.

Murad I was probably the first Ottoman ruler who
bore the title of Sultan. The policy of *sürgün* (settling
nomads on farm lands) was adopted in his time, involving shifts of population from one district to another.
The Islamization of conquered peoples gained momentum, facilitated by the levy (*devshirme*) of Christian
boys into the service of the new state, apparently introduced in the fourteenth century.

Expansion continued under Bayezid (1389-1402) as
the Ottoman armies conquered Macedonia and Bulgaria
(1396) and subjugated several Muslim emirates in Asia
Minor. By this time the Ottoman possessions were organized into two administrative regions (*beylerbeyliks*) —
Anatolia (Asia) and Rumelia (Europe). The Ottoman
expansion alarmed the Christian powers, but division
among them made joint defense impossible. At last, on
the initiative of Pope Boniface IX, an anti-Ottoman
crusade was organized. The Christian soldiers, led by
the Hungarian king, Sigismund, were crushed at Nicopo-
lis (1396). The Ottomans then laid siege to Constantinople, occupied Thessaly, seized Konya, invaded Hungary, and defeated and conquered various Turkish
principalities in Anatolia. But their march was momentarily stopped by Tamerlane's invasion of Anatolia.

The War with Tamerlane and Civil Strife. Aided
and encouraged by some dispossessed Anatolian emirs,
Tamerlane's Mongol forces defeated the Ottomans and
their allies at Ankara (1402) and restored the old Turkish principalities. The Mongols captured the Sultan, and
the resultant anarchy shook the Ottoman Empire. The
Byzantines took advantage of the situation to capture
Salonika, and the Venetians defeated the Turks at Gallipoli. In the meantime the difficulties encounted elsewhere compelled Tamerlane to withdraw from Anatolia,
and Mehmed I (1413-1421) emerged victorious from
the bloody struggle for succession (1402-1413). He

punished those emirs of Asia Minor who had collaborated with the Mongols, checked the Venetians, and
compelled the ruler of Wallachia to pay tribute. Mehmed
was less successful in stamping out religious and social
movements, such as that led by Sheykh Badr al-Din,
eminent Ottoman jurist, author of Sufi * (Muslim mysticism) works and himself a Sufi heretic who propagated
the idea of common ownership. After his capture and
execution his followers were dispersed, eventually joining such orders as Safawiyya and Bektashiyya. (*See
Reading No. 6.*)

Murad II (1421-1451) managed to suppress his domestic enemies and to inflict important defeats on the
Albanians, Greeks, and Rumanians. Byzantium was
forced to surrender some of the Black Sea ports to the
Turks and, like Serbia and Wallachia, to pay tribute to
the Sultan. The Turks recaptured Salonika and quelled
the unruly elements in Asia Minor. They won a great
victory at Varna, November, 1444, over the crusading
army inspired by Pope Eugene IV and led by the
Transylvanian, Jan Hunyadi, and King Vladislav of
Poland and Hungary. The Turks surged deep into
Greece and in 1446 captured Corinth. Only the Albanian
hero, Skanderbeg (George Kastriotis), successfully resisted the Turks, continuing to hold a large portion of
the rugged Albanian mountains under his sway.

The Fall of Constantinople. A new epoch in Ottoman history opened with the ascendancy of Mehmed
II (1451-1481), a complex personality, ruthless and
calculating, yet magnanimous and cultivated. He spoke
five languages and patronized learning and the arts.
Mehmed the Conqueror read Greek and had at his court
a Greek chronicler, and the Italian painter Gentile Bellini
was invited to do a portrait of him.

The first fixed aim in Mehmed's mind was to conquer
the Byzantine capital. After thorough military prepa-
rations, on Tuesday, May 29, 1453, in the early hours
of the morning, his vast army launched an assault by
land and sea. Emperor Constantine XI Palaeologus
Dragases died sword in hand. The fall of the famous
city was a momentous event in modern history, seriously

* Sufism at various stages has had the connotation of rebelling
   against orthodoxy and hence against authority.

affecting subsequent developments in Europe and the Middle East.

Constantinople made a tremendous impression on the Turks. Tursun Beg, secretary of the Sultan's council, who wrote a biography of Mehmed; the chronicler Ashik-pashazade; and the historian Sa'd al-Din wrote ecstatically about the beauty and majesty of the city. Ashik-pashazade described in detail the 51 days of struggle for the city, its wealth and splendor, the killing and the plunder, and the city's girls. The sultan entered the city, went to the Church of the Holy Wisdom (Hagia Sophia or Aya Sofya), and facing Mecca offered a prayer: "I testify that there is no God but God. I testify that our lord Muhammad is the Prophet of God."

Mehmed the Conqueror was remembered not only for his military achievements, but also for the many fundamental measures he introduced in the Ottoman system of government. The legislative act of 1476 (*kanunname*) defined the functions of state officials. The Sultan codified feudal relations, supplied an organization for the *ulema,* expanded and improved the army, established a navy, and built numerous mosques and public projects. The religious policy toward the non-Muslim scripturarians—Christians, Jews, and others who had their own scriptures—though not original with him, was spelled out more explicitly.

The overthrow of Byzantium marked the beginning of the Ottoman Empire. The Turks were henceforth in a position to conquer the Balkans, to convert the Black Sea into their lake, and to advance into Central Europe, the Ukraine, the Caucasus, Arabia, and North Africa. Momentarily repulsed by Jan Hunyadi at Belgrade (1456), the Turks conquered the Despotate of Serbia three years later, then the duchy of Athens, the principality of Morea, and finally the Greek state of Trebizond (1461). The kingdom of Bosnia fell to them in 1463 and Hercegovina in 1482. In 1475 the Sultan's forces subdued the Genoese colonies in the Crimea and reduced the Tatar Khanate to a tributary province. Khan Mengli Ghirey was, however, allowed considerable local autonomy, and his subjects, being Muslims, were accorded special treatment. Wallachia agreed to pay tribute to the sultan (1476), and after the death of Skanderbeg the Turks subjugated the Albanians (1479). An Ottoman landing on the Italian shore at Otranto (1480) was more spectacular than significant. In repeated attacks the sultan failed to capture the island of Rhodes from the Knights of St. John.

Mehmed's death in 1481 led to a struggle for succession between his sons, Bayezid and Jem. Bayezid won out and ruled from 1481 to 1512. Jem took refuge with the Knights of St. John, and later with the Pope, and his presence abroad led to international intrigue against the Ottoman Empire. His death in Rome under peculiar circumstances relieved the sultan of anxiety and enabled him to concentrate on imperial affairs. He withdrew the Ottoman troops from Italy, and in 1492 sent an army into the Alps. Victory over the Venetians at Lepanto (1499) gave the Ottomans additional Aegean islands and a firmer hold on Morea. The sultan repulsed the Egyptian Mameluks at Adana and with the help of the Khan of the Crimea reduced Moldavia to vassalage (1501).

The Persian Challenge. Two important developments bore great portent for the future of the Ottoman Empire: the emergence of Russia from under the Tatar yoke and the founding of Safavid rule in Persia. While Russia did not pose a serious problem for the Turks until the end of the seventeenth century, the challenge presented by Persia was almost immediate. In the name of Persian traditionalism and Shiite sectarianism the Safavids rallied the people of Persia into a cohesive state, and in so doing they split the Muslim world. Henceforth the Turks, checked by the Persians in the East, pushed into the Arab world. The period witnessed a shift in the Ottoman cultural orientation from Persian to Arab traditions and modes.

The Sunnite Turks and Shiite Persians came to represent religious and national antipodes. They waged a number of wars against each other until the borders between their two states were fixed in the first half of the eighteenth century. The revival of Shiism stirred up popular ferment in Anatolia, and the Ottoman sultans had to take drastic action to stamp out this subversive force. Sultan Selim I (1512-1520) contended vigorously

with both Shiite sectarianism in Anatolia and the Persian
bid to dominate the Middle East.

Selim and Suleiman. The rule of Selim I was brief
but eventful. Remembered as a great warrior, he extended Ottoman territorial possessions in Asia and
entered Africa. He crushed the supporters of Shiism in
Anatolia and took Azerbayjan and Kurdistan from Persia.
Even more important were his conquests of Syria (1516)
and Egypt (1517). In acquiring Egypt, the sultan gained
economic and strategic advantages for the empire and
allegedly took away the caliphal prerogatives from Caliph
Mutawakkil, the descendant of the Abbasids who had
found refuge in the court of the Mameluks after the
Mongol conquest of Baghdad in 1258. Did Mutawakkil
surrender his prerogatives and symbols of caliphal office
to Selim? If he did, did he do so voluntarily or under
duress? The first document (*Fetihname*) concerning
Selim's conquest of Egypt does not mention the caliphate,
and the Turkish annals do not speak of the caliph or
a caliphate. "The Caliphate became the living topic only
in the time of Abdul Hamid."

The brutality with which Selim handled his opponents
won him the name "the Grim." He vigorously suppressed
every form of opposition to the established order, including the religious movement led by one Jelal, who had
proclaimed himself the *mahdi* ('the divinely guided).*
From this time on many movements in Ottoman history,
regardless of their real origins and orientations, were
dubbed Jelali movements.

Some identify Selim as an early Pan-Islamist who saw
the Empire's future not in Europe, but in the religiously
homogeneous Middle East. He apparently toyed with the
idea of making Arabic the official language of the empire.
When he died in 1520 Selim left to his son, Suleiman, a
stable state, a powerful army, and a full treasury. The
succession was not contested, which was a good omen.

Suleiman the Magnificent. The Ottoman Empire
attained the greatest political and spiritual power in the
time of Suleiman the Magnificent, known to the Turks
as the Lawgiver (1520-1566). (*See Reading No. 1.*)
Constantinople (Turkish: Istanbul) became the brilliant

---

* Another important social-religious insurrection was led by
   Shah Kuli (Shaitan Kuli).

metropolis of the Empire. The sultan was a builder on a grand scale. The Venetian Ambassador, Bernardo Navagero, in 1553, observes that "The Turkish Court is a superb sight, and most superb is the Sultan himself. One's eyes are dazzled by the gleam of gold and jewelry. Silk and brocade shimmer in flashing rays. What strikes one about Suleiman the Magnificent is not the flowing robes or his high turban. He is unique among the throng because his demeanor is that of a truly great superior." A man of great accomplishments, Suleiman was not without faults, one of which was a weakness for women. Feminine guile prompted Suleiman to kill two of his sons and to leave the throne to the least deserving of the survivors. Of all his wives, the most notorious was the daughter of a Russian priest, Khurrem Sultana—known to posterity as Roxelana. But the Sultan's military successes and legislative acts far outweighed his human foibles and political failures.

In 1521 Suleiman won Belgrade from the Hungarians and made it an impregnable frontier fortress from which he could invade Hungary and Austria. A year later he took Rhodes. The Knights of St. John were permitted to go to Crete, whence they eventually reached Malta. In 1526 Suleiman's army routed the Hungarians at Mohacs. Suleiman wrote that night: "We are resting at Mohacs where we have buried 20,000 Hungarian infantry and 4,000 of the cavalry." Had it not been for the troubles in the east, where the Persians had taken Tabriz, the Ottomans would have advanced deeper into Central Europe. Instead they were obliged to fight on two fronts, but within a few years Suleiman recaptured Tabriz and seized Baghdad.

After Mohacs, one part of Hungary fell to the Turks and another to the Austrians. The struggle for control of Hungary led to a number of wars between the Ottoman and Austrian rulers during the ensuing century. In 1529 Suleiman launched his campaign for the conquest of Vienna, an undertaking of enormous magnitude and logistical problems. Failing on this occasion, Suleiman in the 1530's made plans for another attempt. In 1535 he concluded a treaty, the so-called Capitulations, with Francis I of France, who was also an enemy of the Habsburgs. By the Capitulations Francis obtained special

trading, religious, and consular privileges in Egypt and
the Ottoman Empire.

The Wars on Sea and Land. Ottoman ships plied
the waters of the Mediterranean, the Red Sea, and the
Indian Ocean under the empire's greatest admirals. One
of them, Piri Reis, is renowned for extending imperial
rule to Yemen, Aden and the Persian Gulf, and for
exploring the Indian Ocean. He produced an atlas of
the seas. The Sultan converted the corsairs of the Bar-
bary coast—the rulers of Tunis, Algeria, and Tripoli—
into a wing of the fleet. The famous corsair chief, Khair
al-Din Barbarossa, who was said to have been of Greek
origin, gradually attained command of the imperial navy.
Another distinguished sailor, Admiral Turgut Reis, died
in 1565 during an unsuccessful attack on Malta.

While the Turkish and French navies in the Mediterranean challenged the fleet of Emperor Charles V, the
Turkish land forces pressed against the Habsburgs in
Hungary. The Ottoman fleet under Khair al-Din raided
the coastline of Europe and in 1538 won a great victory
over the fleet of the Holy League, consisting of the
Emperor, the Pope, and Venice, commanded by the
famous Genoese admiral, Andrea Doria. In 1542 French
and Ottoman forces seized Nice. The death of Barbarossa
in 1546 and the desertion of the French compelled
Suleiman to conclude a five years' truce with the Emperor in 1547.

Meanwhile, the death of John Zapolya, the sultan's
candidate for the throne of Hungary, led in 1540 to
another Turkish invasion of Central Europe. In 1547
Emperor Ferdinand agreed to pay tribute in exchange
for a part of Hungary, to renounce his claims to the
rest of the country, and to recognize the Turkish candidate as prince of Transylvania. A new war broke out
with Austria in the early fifties, but Suleiman was forced
to conclude an armistice in 1553 in order to send his
armies against the Persians. After conquering Armenia
and Georgia, he signed a treaty of peace with Persia
(1555) and turned his attention once more to problems
in Europe. Formal peace between Austria and the Ottoman Empire was finally concluded in 1562.

The peace with Austria was short-lived. In 1564 Emperor Maximilian II refused to pay tribute, and the sultan undertook a powerful offensive in Central Europe. The sultan's death during the siege of Szigeth was kept secret until his son Selim II, known as "the Sot," took over the reins of power. While signs of decay had already been apparent in the Ottoman state in the time of Suleiman, they now came into full expression.

— 3 —

GOVERNMENT AND
THE ARMED FORCES

The Ottoman political system was perfected during the fifteenth and the sixteenth centuries. According to Albert H. Lybyer it consisted of two parts: the Ruling Institution made up of converted Muslims and the Muslim Institution made up of born Muslims. Arnold Toynbee and H. A. R. Gibb attribute the unity and strength of the Ottoman Empire to that system. Everything went well so long as those of one institution did not infringe on the functions of the other.

Included in the Ruling Institution were "the sultan and his family, the officers of his household, the executive officers of the government, the standing army composed of cavalry and infantry and a large body of young men who were being educated for service in the standing army, the court, and the government." The Ruling Institution controlled all the functions of government with the exception of justice. Most of those who belonged to the Ruling Institution entered it as the sultan's slaves. Hence they were referred to as the Slaves of the Porte (*Kapi Kullari*).

Included in the Muslim Institution were "the educators, priests, juriconsults, and judges of the empire and all those who were in training for such duties," as well as *dervishes* and *sayyids* (descendants of the Prophet). These persons, all Muslim born, were in charge of Muslim learning, religion, and law.

In a recent article N. Itzkowitz offers a theory based upon career lines rather than religious origins. As he sees it, the Ottoman system rested "on at least three pillars," which correspond to the three main career lines in the empire: bureaucrats (*kalemiye*), military personnel (*seyfiye*), and cultural elements (*ilmiye*). The last of these apparently included both the "religious" and the "academic" people. He recognizes that in the sixteenth century there was also a fourth, the Palace career group, which comprised the leading products of the Palace School system.

Analysis of the Ottoman institutional organization by Stanford Shaw is similar to that of Itzkowitz. He describes the Ottoman power as vested in the imperial officialdom, including the sultan's family and palace officials (*mülkiye*) headed by the Sultan; the military personnel (*seyfiye*); the administrative cadre (*kalemiye*); and the religious leaders (*diniye*).

Recruitment of Christians. There has been a tendency to attribute the greatness of the Ottoman Empire mainly to "the presence of men of Christian origin in positions of importance," and to see the decline of the empire in the replacement of the converted Muslims by the Muslim born. This, of course, is an oversimplification of a greatly complicated problem.

Nonetheless, the recruitment of Christian "slaves" into the government did help to swell the Ottoman ranks and to perpetuate their state. The "slaves" taken into the imperial service were considered "the property of the masters." The Sacred Law divided mankind into free and bond men, or into the Domain of Islam (*Dar al-Islam*), or the World of Truth," and the Domain of War (*Dar al-Harb*). Only the inhabitants of the latter could be enslaved. It was the duty of Muslims to wage "Holy War" (*jihad*)—a war for the faith—against the infidels and thereby to expand their domain.

Although slaves could be born and live within the domain of Islam, their supply was limited as a result of emancipation and the "free status of children born by slave women to free masters." The slaves, therefore, had to come in the main from outside. The Sacred Law provided that one-fifth of any booty, including prisoners, should go to the ruler. Slaves, who were captured in war, purchased, or received as gifts, were put into service as eunuchs, oarsmen for naval vessels, or as ordinary workers.

Originally the Ottomans relied primarily on volunteer fighters for their military force. But as time passed, this source diminished, and it became necessary to use slaves as soldiers. In this connection the *devshirme* was introduced. Youths were drafted, converted, and trained for government or military work, and gradually they replaced the free Muslims in the Ruling Institution.

The Sultan and the Caliph. The Ottoman government was a theocratic monarchy at the head of which stood the sultan-caliph, who professed to rule according to the principles of Muslim Sacred Law (*Sharia*). (*See Reading No. 3.*) Many of the ideas upon which the Ottoman monarchy was built came from ancient Arabia, Persia, and Greece. The actual protocol of relations between the sovereign and his subjects in an Islamic community was drawn up in the period of the caliphate; the caliph's duties and functions were prescribed, and even the conditions under which he could be deposed were established. The sultan inherited many of the duties that once belonged to the caliph. Apart from the obligation to maintain Islamic order, the sultan was responsible for the maintenance of peace and order, and while theoretically restricted in his actions, he was in fact an absolute ruler, no less so than the Abbasid caliphs before him.

As heirs of Byzantium, the Ottoman sultans inherited many Byzantine institutions, legal practices, and forms of statecraft. Historians trace the elaborate Ottoman bureaucracy, the notion of *kanun* (law) framing, and the Sultan's legal initiative (*urf*) to Byzantine influence. While some authors, such as Nicolae Iorga, exaggerate the extent of Byzantine influence on the Ottoman government, others, such as Gibb and Fuad Köprülü, consider it far less significant.

The first ten Ottoman sultans were exceptionally able. Nearly all who followed Suleiman the Magnificent were incompetent. Because there was an absence of an effective principle governing succession, a sultan's death was followed by a struggle among his sons and relatives for the throne. Mehmed the Conqueror issued a legislative act which provided that sultans for the good of the state should murder their brothers and ensure the peaceful passing of the throne from father to son. A regulation issued in 1617 specified that the succession should go "to the eldest surviving male member of the imperial house," and hence uncles and cousins rather than sons generally succeeded to the imperial throne. The fact that sons of previous sultans were confined to special quarters and spent their time in the company of harem women and eunuchs explains why there were so many weak rulers.

The Palace. (*See Reading No. 2.*) The sultan's palace or household consisted of the Harem, the Inside Service, and the Outside Service. The Harem was that part of the palace in which the sultan kept his children, wives (*kadins*), and concubines. (*See Reading No. 5.*) Each wife had her own living quarters, gardens, courts, and staff. Those who bore sons enjoyed a higher title than those who bore girls, and the one that bore the first son was given a special title. The highest-ranking woman in the imperial household was the mother of the sultan, the *valide sultan*. Below the wives were women slaves, the highest being the privileged ones (*gediklis*) from whom the wives were chosen. After the fifteenth century, women of the Harem frequently exercised a powerful influence on the sultan and on state affairs. From the sixteenth century on the sultans had no wives, but only concubines.

The Inside and Outside Services. The domain of the pages and white eunuchs in the palace constituted the Inside Service, which was under the control of the Officer of the Gate (*kapi agasi*), the highest-ranking white eunuch. The Inside Service provided pages, sultan's guards, and kitchen provisions, made up the Privy Chamber, and supplied the Head Valet, Confidential Secretary, sword bearer, and several other important officials.

The Outside Service—the domain of the black eunuchs —was not concerned exclusively with affairs in the palace. From the eighteenth century on, black eunuchs replaced white eunuchs as the guardians of the Harem. The head of the black eunuchs—comptroller of the maid-

ens (*kizlar agasi*)—was, after the sultan and the grand
vezir, the highest Ottoman official, holding the rank of
vezir (or pasha) with three horsetails (*tughs*). The Outside Service was also concerned with the administration,
the army, and the learned professions, and the black
eunuchs contributed several generals of the standing
army, the standard bearer, the intendant of the door
keepers, etc. The most important of them bore the rank
of *agha* (*aghas* of the stirrup). Black eunuchs were in
charge of the imperial gardens, mint, food supplies, and
messengers. Numerous minor officials responsible for
architecture, public works, pastures, the water supply,
and much else, were also members of the Outside Service. (*See Reading No. 5.*)

Central Government. After 1453 Constantinople
(Istanbul) became the Ottoman capital, and the palace
and government were established there. The highest-
ranking official in the government, after the sultan, was
the grand vezir. He appointed a number of prominent
officials, from the sixteenth century on commanded the
army in time of war, and conducted government affairs
with the assistance of several high aides. The building
which housed the offices of the grand vezir and heads of
internal and foreign affairs is referred to in Western
literature as the Sublime Porte (a translation of *Bab-i
Ali*—the High Gate). There is uncertainty as to what the
"Gate" was, but the term Sublime Porte is used in Europe
in much the same sense that the Cabinet of St. James is
used for the British Government.

Until the sixteenth century, the most important state
officials after the grand vezir were two *kadi askers*
(judges) and two *defterdars* (heads of finance), one
being in charge of the Asian and the other of the European possessions of the empire. Since the grand vezir
was frequently absent from the capital because of his
participation in wars and in other activities, at first two
and later as many as nine vezirs of the dome* were appointed to take temporary charge of specific affairs.

In the sixteenth century, however, the grand vezir
conducted state affairs with the aid of the imperial council (*divan*). The *divan* passed on petitions, issued de-

* So called because they met in a domed chamber in the
palace.

cisions promulgated by official orders (*fermans*) and diplomas (*berats*), and made special pronouncements. After the sixteenth century, the imperial council increasingly acquired the character of a high court of justice, over which the grand vezir presided. By the eighteenth century, important changes took place in the relative importance of different government offices.

The period of Reformation, or *Tanzimat* (*see Chapter 14*), in the nineteenth century brought fundamental changes in government. In certain cases the *Tanzimatists* attempted to graft European institutions onto the existing Ottoman system, and in others they introduced entirely new institutions. In 1835 the department of the *kahya* was transformed into the ministry of civil affairs, which became the ministry of the interior two years later. The departments of the *reis efendi* and the *defterdar* became ministries of foreign affairs and finance respectively. For a short while after 1837 the grand vezir was called the prime minister and presided over a privy council created by the sultan.

Not until the beginning of the nineteenth century do we encounter the first Muslim *dragoman* (interpreter), Yahya Efendi (a convert). In 1833 Mahmud II established a government translation bureau for the training of interpreters and linguists. By 1835, when the Ottomans reopened the embassies abroad which had been closed since the time of Selim II, there were already trained interpreters to staff them. Some of those who received linguistic training later became prominent in Ottoman political life, such as Mustafa Reshid Pasha, who served as ambassador in Paris and was primarily responsible for the *Hatt-i Sherif* of 1839, the first Ottoman "Bill of Rights." The French-educated Ahmed Vefik held the post of grand vezir twice and was president of the parliament in 1876.

Regional Government. The Ottoman Empire was subdivided into provinces administered directly from the capital, tributary territories, and lands which enjoyed a special status. In Europe, for example, Hungary and Transylvania were kingdoms, Dubrovnik (Ragusa) a republic, Wallachia and Moldavia principalities, Montenegro (*Karadag*) a theocratic principality, and Mt. Athos an ecclesiastical republic.

Most of the Balkan provinces, as well as Egypt, Syria (Damascus), and Iraq (Baghdad), were "directly administered" by officials of the Porte. Each province submitted annual payments (*irsaliye*) to the Sultan. The Arab provinces paid these sums regularly. The Ghirey khans of Crimea, whose subjects were descended from the Golden Horde, were almost free from outside interference. The Sherif of Mecca held a similar status, and Medina, after Mecca the most sacred city of the Muslims, was administered by a black eunuch, appointed by the sultan from his palace. Otherwise Mecca and Medina formed a single "province" under an Ottoman governor. In Algeria, Tunisia, and Tripoli, elected beys or deys were largely independent in administering local affairs. They sent contributions to the sultan in cash, ships, and men, but unlike the vassal Christian lands which paid tribute to the sultan, the Muslim possessions received gifts from him. The Yemen was a distinct entity, at times independent of Ottoman control. Several other communities and islands were governed in a special way. In accordance with Ottoman tribal policy, the tribal chiefs in Egypt, Syria, Kurdistan, Anatolia, and Albania paid tribute in exchange for freedom.

Until 1517 the Ottoman Empire was divided into Asian and European military and administrative regions (*beylerbeyliks* of Anatolia and of Rumelia respectively). As the Imperial territories expanded, new regions (*beylerbeyliks* or *vilayets* or *pashaliks*) were constituted. In the sixteenth century there were nine of them, each headed by a governor general (*beylerbey*) appointed by an imperial decree. As a rule a governor general was granted one of the largest landed fiefs (*khass*), and the man who held the position bore the rank of pasha (at first with two, and later with three horsetails) and was given the title of *vezir*.

Each governor general had his own staff and met with its members in an assembly (*divan*). The most important of his subordinates was the *defterdar*, the regional director of finances. The governor general was authorized to grant small landed fiefs and was in charge of the political and military affairs of his territory. Each region was divided into provinces (*sanjak*) headed by governors (*sanjakbeys*), who were responsible to the governor general. The local judge (*kadi*) possessed extensive powers and was one of the most honored members of the provincial government. The governors directed military and civil affairs in the provinces.

Local Government. The provinces were divided into judicial districts (called *kadilik*) consisting of one or more communes (*nahiye*). The head of a judicial district was a Muslim judge (*kadi*), and the head of a commune, a prefect (*subashi, voyvoda*) who represented the sultan in conduct of administrative and military affairs. In some European districts, there were also Christian representatives (e.g., *knez, kochibashi*), but the exact relationship between them and the deputy governors is yet to be ascertained. A military officer (*serasker* or *cheribashi*), directly subordinated to the governor, commanded the armed forces in one or more districts.

The smallest administrative entities were cities (*shehir*), small towns (*kasaba*), market places (*bazar*), and villages (*kariye*). The cities and small towns were divided into sections and quarters (organized on the basis of confessions or occupations). Foreigners usually lived in separate quarters. Local government in the Ottoman Empire was diversified to meet special situations and needs. The first attempts to improve and modernize local government were undertaken in the time of Selim III. In 1845 Reshid Pasha, the grand vezir, organized the local administration into prefectures and departments under salaried officials in place of farmers and fiefholders. These reforms did not go far enough. The councils (*mejlis*) which were attached to governors (*valis*) of territories (*vilayets*) and provinces (*sanjaks*) neither represented the views of the governed nor curbed "the arbitrary acts of governors."

Armed Forces. The Ottoman armed forces consisted of feudal, standing, and auxiliary contingents. Until the end of the sixteenth century, the feudal army was the principal military arm of the empire.

The Feudal Army. Recipients of landed fiefs (*timars*) were obliged to render military service by providing soldiers and serving themselves, or, in some instances, to make financial payments in lieu of such service. Originally, the fiefs were granted by the governor generals, who issued diplomas to that effect. The legislative code (*kanun name*) of 1530 reserved this right for the central government although governor generals were still permitted to make recommendations in petitions to the Porte for grants of small fiefs.

The fiefholder (*timarli*) kept his fief as long as he fulfilled his military duty and did not commit a criminal act; he sustained his military duty with income obtained from his peasant tenants. The number of mounted and equipped men (*jebeli*) that a fief holder was obliged to contribute depended on the amount of income he received from the fief. The fief holder himself and the men he supplied were known as *Sipahis*—the feudal cavalrymen. On a provincial level they were under the command of the governor (*sanjak bey*), and their immediate commanding officer was the *alay bey*, whom they elected for life and gave a standard and a drum. Next in rank came the *cheribashis* or *subashis*, who were chosen from the ranks of the *zaims*, the holders of fiefs that yielded high incomes (*see Chapter 5*) and certain other officers.

Janissaries. (*See Reading No. 4.*) The recruiting of Christian youth (*devshirme*) at first occurred every four years, and, later, more often. The most promising of the recruited Christian children were selected as pages (*ich oghlan*) and trained in one of the imperial palaces to become the sultan's personal attendants. Most of the other "foreign boys" (*ajemi oghlan*) became members of the standing infantry—the Janissaries (*yeni-cheri*, or "new troops").

Historians believe that the Janissary corps was founded in the fourteenth century, but not formally organized until the time of Murad II. The Janissaries were closely connected with the Bektashi order and were sometimes called the Bektashi soldiery. The corps consisted of 196 companies (*orta,* or center) of various sizes, divided into three divisions—*seghmen, jema'at,* and *bölük.* The largest was the *jema'at* division, which was made up of 101 companies, and the smallest, the *seghmen,* of 34 divisions. Each company was divided into smaller units of *odes, ortas,* and *bölüks.* A Janissary group was commanded by an *agha,* under whom came a number of lower-ranking officers. In the second half of the fifteenth century there were about 10,000 Janissaries; their number rose under Suleiman to 12,000. In time of peace the Janissaries maintained order in urban centers, served as escorts and security guard, and watched the principal gates of the town's fortresses. In time of war they served as infantry, taking the central position in battle formation and protecting the sultan.

The Janissaries were educated in the spirit of militant Islam, and until the sixteenth century they lived a life of celibacy. The Janissaries enjoyed many privileges, and some even rose to high positions in the imperial government. But they were also the first to manifest dissatisfaction with the slave form of government. As early as 1568 Selim II was compelled to grant them "the privilege of enrolling their sons in the corps." The *devshirme* was probably abolished in 1637 although slave apprentices were employed as late as 1750, if not later.

Special Corps. The introduction of firearms in the fifteenth century resulted in the organization of three special corps of the "foreign boys"—the gunners (*topchus*), gun-carriage drivers (*top arabajis*), and armorers (*jebejis*). The latter were primarily concerned with the repair and manufacture of arms and munitions, but they also guarded army transport and stores. The special corps were likewise commanded by aghas.

Finally, the Ottoman standing army included six cavalry divisions, most of which came into existence before the Janissaries. There is reason to believe that in the time of Suleiman the Magnificent cavalry were more numerous than the Janissary troops. In peacetime, cavalrymen worked as scribes, tax collectors, and clerks.

Auxiliary Forces. There were many auxiliary organizations which in exchange for land grants or tax exemptions, or both, performed military duties as special cavalry (*müsellems*), foot soldiers (*yaya* or *piyade*), guardians of the fortresses, scouts, munition carriers, and armed nomads (*yürüks*). Like the feudal army, many of these auxiliaries lost their importance or became extinct in the later period of the empire's history. The Ottomans used Christians for military and policing pur-

poses from the very beginning. The two particularly well
known Christian military organizations were *voynuks*
and *martolos*. The *voynuks* served in the sultan's stables
and cared for horses. The ordinary *voynuks* were given
land (*bashtina*) and granted full or partial exemption
from taxes. Their communities possessed broad autonomy. Lower *voynuk* commanders (*legatori*) were Christians, while the higher (*cheribashi* or *voynuk bey*) were
usually Muslims.

There were still other kinds of Christian soldiers and
para-military units, such as falconers, makers of arrows,
peasants recruited to repair fortresses, guards (*serbenji*)
of bridges, roads and mountain passes, and persons who
cared for horses at way stations (*menzil-hâne*). Most of
the Christian auxiliaries were disbanded after the sixteenth century.

Military Decline. The Ottoman territorial losses
after the sixteenth century, which wiped out many landed
fiefs, and the development of gunpowder in the mid-
sixteenth century caused reductions of the feudal cavalry.
In order to build a more reliable and disciplined army, it
became necessary to pay troops with money rather than
with fiefs. The result was the expansion of the Janissary
corps.

After the defeat at Vienna in 1683 and the military
reverses that followed, the Ottoman leaders recognized
for the first time the superiority of European arms. In
the eighteenth century there was talk about military
reforms, and French instructors were hired to help reform the military organization. Both Abdul Hamid I
(1774-1789) and Selim III (1789-1808) introduced
measures aimed at Westernization of the military. Selim
III wrote to the French King, Louis XVI, requesting his
help in this connection.

Military Reorganization. In 1791 Selim III sent
Ebu Bakir Ratib Efendi to Vienna to study the Austrian
government and military establishment, and in the following year he summoned leading personalities to discuss
reforms. Nearly all those with whom he consulted felt
that military reforms were urgent. The sultan ordered
the establishment of the "new army" (*nizam-i jedid*),
modeled on European armies. Army and navy schools

were opened, and French instructors were employed to teach the Turks modern military science. But the new army had a short life. Selim III was forced to disband it and was himself overthrown in 1808. The military reforms, however, had increased the channels of communication with Europe and thereby swelled knowledge of Western progress.

The wars of Greek independence (1821-1828) completely discredited the Janissaries and the Sipahis. On May 28, 1826, Mahmud II ordered the establishment of a modern army, resembling the earlier "new army." The chief mufti and the *ulema* approved the measure. Before the sultanic regulation could be enforced, the Janissaries rebelled on June 15, but were put down in blood by loyal troops. The Bektashi dervish order, long affiliated with the Janissaries, was dissolved, and its followers dispersed.

The new army, called "the victorious soldiers of Muhammad" (*asakir-i mansure-i muhammediye*), was stationed in Istanbul. Comparable units were to be gradually organized in the provinces. In the meantime the attempts made in 1832 by Muhammad Ali Pasha of Egypt to transform the Ottoman Empire into an Arab empire revealed the superiority of the modern Egyptian army over the troops commanded by Ottoman generals. The Ottoman Empire, on the verge of collapse, was saved by Russia, which wrested from the sultan special privileges in the Straits in the Treaty of Hunkiâr Iskelesi, 1833.

The sultan, in order to escape both the Egyptian enemy and Russian domination, needed a powerful army, and for this he needed European instructors. The English and French had alienated the sultan because of the support they gave the Greeks. The French had also angered him by seizing Algeria, which he considered a part of his empire. The confused sultan turned to Prussia, and in 1835 Captain Helmuth von Moltke (later Field Marshal) and a group of Prussian officers accepted the invitation to modernize the Turkish armed forces.

In this period the naval engineering school, originally founded in 1773, and the military engineering schools, founded in 1793, were reopened. A military music school and a military academy were established in

1831 and 1834, respectively. A *serasker* replaced the *agha* as the new commander-in-chief of the armed forces. The *Hatt-i Sherif of Gülhane* (1839) provided for what was to be a fair system of recruitment of troops by declaring that it was the duty "of all inhabitants to furnish soldiers." The system was not implemented; only a few Christians were admitted into the Ottoman military system.

The military reorganization law adopted in 1841 provided for the organization of the army into five corps and the conscription of soldiers by drawing lots for five years of active duty and seven years of reserve duty, but the non-Muslims still remained largely excluded from the armed forces. Although in 1855 the poll tax was abolished and permission to bear arms was granted to citizens of all denominations, the opening of military service to Christians remained on paper. The *Hatti-i Hümâyun* regulation of 1856 once again promised equal liability of Muslims and non-Muslims to military service. But as it turned out the Christians preferred, and were encouraged, to pay an exemption tax (*bedel*) in lieu of military service.

The character of the Ottoman armed forces was fundamentally transformed after the 1850's. Modern military tactics and organization, as well as European military equipment, were introduced. After 1878 German influence became increasingly predominant, and from the 1880's on the Turkish army was trained by German instructors. General K. von der Goltz was responsible for the modernization of the Turkish army that vanquished the Greeks in the war of 1897. On the eve of the First World War General Liman von Sanders, the head of the German military mission, was virtually in command of the Turkish armed forces.

The Navy. The Ottoman Empire did not develop a navy until the fifteenth century. In command of the navy was a lord high admiral (*kapudan pasha*). The first sailors, called *levends* (*levantino*), were originally recruited from seafaring Greeks, Dalmatians, and Albanians. They were poorly trained and disloyal, and in lieu of payment for their services they shared the captured booty. Eventually companies of Janissaries, feudal

Sipahis, and special infantrymen served on naval vessels. At the end of the sixteenth century still other elements, such as tax-exempted and privileged nomads (*müsellemas* and *yürüks*), were employed by the navy.

The Ottoman navy achieved prominence for the first time during the siege of Constantinople and the conversion of the Black Sea into an Ottoman lake during the second half of the fifteenth century. After a period of relative inactivity it distinguished itself again during the reign of Suleiman the Magnificent, when it attained its greatest power and produced the ablest admirals. (*See Chapter 2.*)

The Aegean islands were organized into a vilayet of the Aegean or the Mediterranean (*vilayet bahri sefid*) and divided into provinces (*sanjaks*) under governors (*sanjak beys*) called the "*sea beys*" (*derya beyleri*).

In a race with the Portuguese for the domination of the Red Sea and the Indian Ocean, Suleiman succeeded in extending the Ottoman empire to Aden, and established his control over the eastern coast of the Red Sea and parts of the western coast. After his death, the Ottoman navy began to decline, and at Lepanto in 1571 it suffered a crushing defeat in battle with the Christian fleet, commanded by Don Juan of Austria.

Galleys made up the bulk of the Ottoman navy, with the crews consisting of men-at-arms, seamen, and rowers. With the decline of the navy and the development of gunnery, galleys were abandoned in favor of oarless sailing ships, and the use of Janissaries and *sipâhîs* was discontinued.

At the zenith of its power in the sixteenth century the Ottoman navy consisted of ten *maynas* (large galleys, each with a crew of 600), 40 *kadirgas* (medium-sized galleys, each with a crew of 300), one admiral's *bastarda* (with a crew of 800), and many smaller craft. The guns were inefficiently mounted, ordnance procedures defective, the supply system often disorganized, and the officers poorly trained. The Ottomans never solved the problem of provisioning and maintaining a navy.

The Ottomans had to wage war for 25 years (1644-1669) before they were able to take the island of Crete from Venice. The Russian pressure in the Black Sea and demands for security in the Mediterranean after the Peace of Carlowitz (1699) compelled Ahmed III to strengthen the empire's naval power. Half-hearted attempts were made in the eighteenth century to reorganize and modernize the navy. The first serious efforts to develop a first-class navy came under Selim III, though a modern naval engineering school had already been established in 1773. In the Russo-Turkish wars during the eighteenth and nineteenth centuries, the Tsar's navy repeatedly defeated the sultan's. One more effort to bring the navy up to date, on the eve of the First World War, with the assistance of the British Admiral Limpus, bore little fruit.

On August 2, 1914, Turkey and Germany signed a secret military convention, and a few days later the Turks permitted two German warships (the *Göben* and the *Breslau*) to pass in disguise through the straits into the Black Sea. The ships were given Turkish names (*Selim Yavuz* and *Midilli*), and the German Admiral Souchon took over the command of the Turkish navy from Admiral Limpus. Thanks to this German stratagem, the Ottoman navy was able to play a minor role in the First World War.

— 4 —

JUSTICE AND EDUCATION

The Ottoman Empire was a theocratic state in which Muslim sacred law (*sharia*) was the principal law of the land. The sources of the sacred law were the Koran and tradition (*sunnah* and *hadith*), but because they were inadequate to meet all situations, it became necessary to introduce two principles: analogical deduction (*qiyas*) and catholic consent (*ijma'*) The latter was reckoned to be of two kinds, the consensus of the whole community of Islam (*ijma' al-ummah*) and the consensus of the *imams*, the great teachers of the law or leaders of the people (*ijma' al-a'imma*).

Thus it was for the doctors of law (*mujtahids*), on the basis of revealed law and analogy, to rule on many legal questions. However, not all doctors interpreted the law in the same way, and consequently four schools developed, each with its fundamental texts and extensive commentaries. The Ottomans adhered to the Hanafite school (the other Sunni schools are Shafiite, Malikite, and Hanbalite) and complemented their legal system by enactments called *kanuns* (canons), rules and regulations issued by the sultan in the spirit of the sacred law. The Ottoman rulers made use of their own custom and initiative (*urf*) only in fields which the sacred law did not cover.

Besides the Muslim sacred law, the customary law of Oghuz nomads was also operative in certain parts of the Ottoman Empire. The non-Muslims retained their customary and church laws, according to which many family and communal questions were decided, although the parties in dispute could avail themselves of Muslim courts if they wished. Suits involving both Christians and Muslims were tried in Muslim courts.

The Judicial System. The Ottoman judicial system was organized into a hierarchy headed by the two *kadi askers* whose position has already been described. Below them came the *kadis* of a higher grade (the great *Mollas*), who were stationed in the major cities, including 'Istanbul. Next in rank were *kadis* of a lower grade, one of whom was the *kadi* of Baghdad. Smaller districts had ordinary judges and their deputies (*naibs*). Each province (*sanjak*) was divided into a number of judicial districts (*kadilik*), in each of which there was a judge.

Judges in Asia and Egypt were under the jurisdiction of the *kadi asker* of Anatolia, and those of Europe, North Africa, and Crimea under the *kadi asker* of Rumelia. There existed separate Asian, European, and Egyptian judicial services, and judges holding a position in one could not as a rule be transferred to another. Not until after the time of Suleiman the Magnificant did the judges receive sound theological and legal training.

The judges of each service were classified according to several grades. The European service, for example, had nine grades. Until the middle of the eighteenth century, the judges—mainly Turkish-speaking—held their positions for a specific period, usually a year, and had to be re-appointed. They paid a fee for investiture or confirmation. Judicial offices, like others, were farmed out and usually went to the highest bidder. At first, the incomes of judges came from judicial fees and from fiefs (*timars*) they received. After the sixteenth century it seems that their fiefs were taken away from them.

The Ottoman government appointed only the Hanafite judges; where other schools predominated, the local authorities appointed appropriate jurists, and the same was done in Shiite and Druze areas. Each judge appointed one or more deputies (*naibs*), who were confirmed by the *kadi askers*. In addition to judicial work, the judges supervised mosques and religious endowments, appointed instructors in the schools, and watched over the administration as a whole. They served as supervisors of imperial lands and other sources of revenue and as inspectors of courts. They assessed special taxes, took the census of sheep for purpose of taxation, fixed prices for grain and foodstuffs, supervised in some instances the collection of taxes, and investigated irregularities in connection with the ownership of land.

The *muftis* were a special class of practitioners of law. Unlike the judges, who were appointed by the ruler who served at his discretion, the *muftis* were private scholars who received "some measure of official recognition," and, officially, they were not paid. A *mufti* was associated with every city *kadi* and interpreted the sacred law for him and responsible government officials. On request he issued a *fetva* or legal opinion on a specific question. He was trained in a *medrese*. Suleiman the Magnificent supplied an organization for the *muftis,* but it was not as tight as that of the judges. Sultan Mehmed II elevated the *mufti* of Istanbul to the rank of *sheykh ul-islam,* the highest religious official. The *sheykh ul-islam* appointed the *muftis* to all major cities and judicial districts (*kadi-liks*). In addition to interpreting the sacred law and issuing legal opinions, the *sheyk hul-islam* was entrusted with other matters relating to religion and education. In the course of the sixteenth century the *sheykhs* contributed much toward the development of the law, but the actual administration of justice remained in the hands of the *kadi asker.*

Irregularities and abuses were fairly common in the Ottoman judicial system. On various occasions the sultans, especially Suleiman the Magnificent, issued special *kanuns* in an effort to curb corruption. The Ottoman leaders faced greater difficulty in reforming the traditional system of justice than in reforming any other institution. *Kadis* and *muftis* resisted stubbornly anything that threatened their position. The office of grand *mufti,* established in 1826, brought about the "bureaucratization" of the *ulema* and curtailment of their power. This, coupled with the imposition of state control over religious endowments, restricted the financial independence of the *ulema.* Their power was further limited when the state took over the right to appoint teachers, and when the administration of law was entrusted to the minister of justice and appointed judges. Henceforth the grand *mufti,* a government official, had only consultative powers. In 1837 the Council of Justice was founded and later enlarged in membership and given a supervisory function.

In matters of justice, as in many other state affairs, the Turks favored French practices. The French penal code, adjusted to the Muslim penal law, was adopted in 1840, but because of the strong opposition of the *ulema,* a commercial code was not adopted until 1850. In 1847 mixed civil and criminal courts, made up of an equal number of Muslims and European judges, were established to handle cases involving foreigners. This represented a step toward equality as Christian testimony against Muslims was admitted in these courts. The *Hatt-i Hümâyun* of 1856 promised judicial equality for all inhabitants. The new penal code was adopted in 1858, commercial and mixed courts merged in 1860, and commercial and maritime codes introduced in 1861 and 1863 respectively. An important step forward was taken in 1868 with the creation of a Divan of Judicial Ordinances, an improved version of the one-time Council of Justice, and a Council of State, which served as "a high court of appeal in administrative cases." Between 1869 and 1876 there was introduced a new civil code (*Mejelle*—16 volumes, 1869–1876), which remained in force until 1926. This code was "modern in form," but based on the code of sharia law of the Hanafite school. It was principally the work of Ahmed Jevdet Pasha (1822–1895), the historian and jurist.

The short-lived constitution of 1876 promised a modern judicial system, and Sultan Abdul Hamid attempted to improve the judicial system, but as foreign criticism of Turkish justice persisted, the embittered Sultan abandoned the idea.

Education. Education in the Ottoman Empire was in the hands of the Men of Learning (*ulema*), who supplied teachers for the religious elementary (*mekteb*), higher theological (*medrese*), and other schools. While elementary schools were common, secondary schools were located only in larger cities. Both were usually attached to a mosque, though *medrese* was sometimes

founded as an endowment (*vakf*). In the *mekteb* the
pupil learned Arabic script and read the Koran. It was
the *medrese* that produced the *ulema*. Its curriculum
spread over 9 to 12 years and consisted of Arabic language, Islamic theology, and law. Some dervish monasteries (*tekkes*) also maintained schools.

The best Ottoman schools were those associated with
the Palace and founded by Mehmed the Conqueror. (*See
Reading No. 9.*) They were the *ajemi* and *ich oghlan*
schools, which had the restricted function of training
personnel for palace services. These schools educated
pupils in a variety of fields, such as architecture, callig-
raphy, military science, cannon-making and shipbuilding.
According to the historian Tayyar Zadeh Bey, the Sultan
"conceived the idea of rearing and educating in a general school (*mekteb-i 'umumi*) in his palace the type of
valiant soldier and scholarly official which was needed
for all the functions of the empire." In the course of
time the Palace School acquired the character of a
school for government. Barnette Miller notes that the
Palace School "was a greater departure from the theological or *medrese* type of education than the medieval
university was from the monastic and cathedral schools."

The faculty consisted of royal preceptors drawn from
the ranks of the *ulema,* and of a few Christians. Namik
Kemal Bey writes that Mehmed II tried to stop the
flight to Italy of Greek scholars and writers; for example,
his biographer, Critoboulos, a Greek, was attached to
the court.

There were nine schools in the Palace, five preparatory and four vocational, and three preparatory schools
outside the Palace. The full course of training took 15
years. The number of students was small and promotion
slow. The curriculum consisted of the Turkish, Arabic,
and Persian languages, grammar and literature, study of
the Koran, Muslim theology and law, Turkish history,
music, and mathematics (arithmetic and probably alge-
bra). The fact that until the seventeenth century the
Palace School excluded the participation of freeborn
Turks served "to retard the natural development of the
Turkish people for several hundred years." Otherwise

the Palace School was so efficient that it held steadfast even after other Ottoman institutions had begun to decline.

Educational Reforms. The Ottoman educational system was inadequate and backward, benefiting only a few well-to-do subjects. (*See Reading No. 12.*) The Muslim masses had available to them religious education on an elementary school level. But the poor of all faiths were beyond the scope of advanced and formal education. The Christians and Jews had their schools; these were few and sustained by their respective communities. The prominent authoress Halidé Edib observes, however, that "Educationally, the non-Muslim nations fared better than Muslims . . . they were aware of the changes in the outside world, . . . the Muslim peoples, especially the Turks, were always on the battlefield."

Not until the end of the eighteenth century did the Ottomans start to modernize education. By then it was too late to affect the basic course of Ottoman history. It is no surprise that the first modern schools were military. In the reign of Mahmud II (1808–1839) young Ottomans were for the first time sent abroad to study. But the Sultan, who showed great courage in abolishing the Janissaries in 1826, dared not strike at the traditional educational system. Nonetheless, the system of palace education as a remnant of "the slave system of government" had no future. One of the original nine schools, the Galata Saray, though greatly transformed, remained the best Turkish secondary school. Mahmud II also established new secular schools without touching the *medreses*. Dualism thus became characteristic of the nineteenth century period of reforms (the Tanzimat), as the old and new institutions existed side by side. After 1846 several new-type secondary schools, called *rushdiye,* were founded. In a few decades the new secular schools eclipsed the *medreses* as educational centers. With them a new generation of lawyers, doctors, engineers, officers, and public servants arose and became the backbone of growing modernism and secularism.

In 1847 the Council of Public Education, created not long before, was transformed into the Ministry of Education, and the *ulema* were at last stripped of their control over education. From the 1860's on, many modern state and private schools were founded. The example of Robert College, founded in Istanbul by American Protestants in 1863 (*see Reading No. 17*), inspired the government to establish the Imperial Lycée in 1868, modeled on European counterparts.

In the final years of the nineteenth century the school for the training of civil servants (*mülkiye*), established in 1859, and the war college (*harbiye*) were expanded. Nearly two dozen secondary (*rüshdiye*) and higher (*i'dadiye*) schools were opened, including schools for law, finance, fine arts, commerce, civil engineering, police, and medicine. After much discussion the University of Istanbul was finally founded in 1900. Until then the Ottoman Empire had no institution comparable to a Western university. But the complete Westernization of the Turkish educational system did not come about until after the collapse of the Empire and the establishment of Kemalist republican Turkey.

— 5 —

FEUDALISM

The Ottoman state was organized on a system of
military feudalism which had its origins in Persian,
Seljuk, and Byzantine institutions. The sultan was in
charge of all imperial possessions (tax farms and imperial domains, or *havâṣṣi hümâyun*) and had the right
to utilize the country's wealth for his personal advantage and for the benefit of the State Treasury (*hazine-i
amire*). He entrusted leasings (*mukâṭa'as*) to his subordinates for the purpose of exploitation. The distribu-
tion of the leasings was handled by the Sultan's slaves
(*kullar*), who became the ruling class called Ottomans
(*Osmanlilar*). The leasings were not all of the same
kind. The tax farm (*iltizam*) gave the holder (*multezim*)
a part of the revenue (for his management of a given
property), while the rest went to the Treasury. The
steward (*emin*) of another, the least common, kind of
leasing (*emanet*) turned over to the Treasury all revenues he collected. The third type of leasing, the *timar*,
gave the holder (*sipahi*) the entire income from a piece
of property in lieu of a salary for military and administrative services. The recipient of such a leasing managed
it as a representative of the Sultan (*sahid-i arḍ*).

Land Tenure. Arable land was divided into four
categories: state lands (*miri*); the lands of the Sultan
(*khass*); the lands of the Muslim religious endowments
(*vakf*); and private or alodial lands (*mulk*). The Ottoman rulers distributed among military men, in the form
of landed fiefs, most of the arable land in Anatolia and
Europe and in certain Arab districts. The fiefs were
granted for life on condition of military service. Byzan-

44

tium exercised a powerful influence in shaping the
Ottoman system of military fiefs. The holders and the
men they contributed constituted the feudal cavalry
(*sipâhîs*), with their military obligation depending on
the amount of income the fief yielded. (*See Chapter 3.*)
Fiefs which brought an income of from 2,000 to 19,999
akches (*aspres*—pieces of silver) were called *timars*.
Those with incomes of between 19,999 and 99,999
akches were called *ziamets*. A fief with an income over
99,999 *akches* was called a *khass*.

Income from arable lands granted to religious endowments went toward the maintenance of religious, educational, and other social establishments. On occasion the
Sultan made unconditional grants of land to private
individuals. Undistributed lands constituted the imperial
or Sultan's domains, the income from which went to the
State Treasury, and the Palace.

The *timars* were prevalent in the provinces of Anatolia
and Europe, while the *iltizam* or tax farms existed
primarily in the *vilayets* of Egypt, Bagdad, and Basrah.
In the *timar* provinces the lands were divided into landed
fiefs, the holders of which rendered military and other
services to the government in return for the income they
collected. In the *iltizam* provinces the lands were grouped
into tax farms (*iltizams*) usually entrusted to prominent
military men and certain others for supervision and exploitation. The revenues (*saliyane*) from the tax farms
were shared between the local government and the
Treasury. After local costs, including the governor's annual salary, were met, what remained of the collected
revenues was sent to Istanbul.

The collectors (*mütevellis*) of taxes from religious
lands and the tax farmers, after the sixteenth century,
likewise retained a percentage of what they collected.
Taxes and dues collected from the peasants by agents of
the religious endowments were used for the maintenance
of mosques, schools, and other establishments. The taxes
from the undistributed imperial lands went to the State
Treasury and the Sultan's Privy Purse.

Landlords and the Peasants. The most common
landed fief was the *timar*. The holder could not sell it,
pass it on to his heirs, or transfer it to a religious institu-

tion. Nonetheless, the holder normally managed to leave
the fief to his son if the latter was qualified for military
service. Within the fief the holder held properties (*khassa
chiftlik* or *beglik*) which he managed himself. Through
the right of collecting taxes, the fief holder acquired
seigneurial jurisdiction over the peasants on the fief.

The tillers of the soil were peasants, called *rayah**
(flock or subjects) in most of the Empire and *fellahin*
in Egypt. The peasants were entitled to the use of the
land on which they lived, and in this sense they were
effective owners so long as they cultivated the land and
paid taxes. But the rights of the peasants were frequently
ignored, and they themselves were subjected to wanton
exploitation and oppression. Although taxes were fixed
by law and the peasant could, in principle, prefer charges
against his landlord before the Muslim authorities, abuses
associated with the collection of taxes were widespread.

The peasant worked both the land which he was able
to use (*tasarruf*) and the landlord's land. He "owned"
the land on which his house was located and a small
parcel of land adjacent to it. The most important tax
which he paid was a tenth (*ushr* or *haraj*) of his produce, collected in kind at the time of the harvest. The
peasant gave the landlord a seventh or eighth of the yield
of some products and paid fixed taxes on his house,
sheep, and certain other items. Both Muslim and non-
Muslim peasants were obliged to perform a number of
days of free labor (*kulluk*) on the landlord's private
farm. The peasants paid taxes to both their landlords and
to the state, in kind and in money. As a "representative"
of the Sultan, the landlord collected the tax from the
lands owned by peasants and lands which the peasants
were entitled to use.

At first the Turks did not attach peasants to the land,
and the landholder could do no more than compel a
peasant who deserted the land to pay a fee over a number of years in lieu of damages. Later on the peasants
were registered and assigned to a particular fief-holder
and could not voluntarily alter that relationship. One of
the legal regulations (*kanuns*) actually bound peasants

---

* The term is sometimes applied to one of the non-Muslim
   communities or to an individual member of such a community.

to the soil and for all intents and purposes reduced them
to the status of serfs. The feudal lord could, therefore,
compel the peasant to return to the land from which he
fled, though this right lapsed after 15 years. The only
way he could secure freedom was by becoming a city
dweller or by entering military service. The son could
inherit his father's right to use the land on a particular
estate. Any other heir was obliged to pay a special
tax for it. With the landlord's permission the peasant
could sell his right to the use of the given land. Until the
sixteenth century the peasant had the hereditary right to
use the land on which he lived so long as he worked it,
and the landlord was entrusted with the right to collect
taxes from the land so long as he complied with the
conditions on which the fief was granted to him.

Taxes.   State revenues were derived from taxes,
dues, fees, and customs duties, as well as from war booty
and tribute. For purposes of taxation Ottoman subjects
were divided into a military class (*asker*) and a working
class (*rayah*). There were also groups that did not fit
into either category. Some Christians were exempt from
paying taxes and enjoyed special privileges without being
members of the military class. Similarly, the Men of
Learning (*ulema*) were not, strictly speaking, of the
military class, but for purposes of taxation they were
included in that category.

Ottoman taxes were divided into two kinds: *hukuk-i
shariya*, which included land (*ushr, haraj*) and poll
(*jizye*) taxes and certain others, and *rusum-i urfiye*,
taxes assessed by the Sultan, which were mostly of pre-
Ottoman origin. The latter were of several categories:
chift resmi, paid until the sixteenth century by all male
adults; taxes on livestock; fines and marriage fees; trade
imposts; taxes on state monopolies (salt, rice, wax,
candles, soap, sesame, lumber, mining, etc.); cash substitutes (*bedel*) for certain services required from subjects; and fees paid upon the issuance of documents
(*berat, tezkers,* etc.). Many local differences in taxation
can be traced to Byzantine, Hungarian, and other tax
practices.

Although all those who were not members of the
ruling class were classified as the "protected flock"
(*rayah*), Muslims were accorded better treatment than

non-Muslims. This was clearly reflected in Islamic fiscal laws and in discriminatory rates of assessment. According to Lewis, the rates were: "the lowest for Muslims, the highest for *Harbis,* and a medium rate for *Zimmis.* The believer, the hostile infidel, the subject infidel— these were the three recognized categories, and nationality, even political allegiance had no bearing on them." Thus, for example, the Christian peasant paid the state a poll tax (*jizye*) in lieu of military service (or an equivalent as tribute), and the land tax (*haraj*). The two taxes were later merged and the terms used interchangeably.

Historical Role of Feudalism. There has been much discussion about the character of Ottoman feudalism and the part it played in history. The main question is whether Ottoman feudalism fostered or impeded social progress. The "legal" picture so often painted of Ottoman feudalism does not always coincide with the actual one. The situation is complicated by the fact that the long existence of Ottoman feudalism and its adaptations to regional needs resulted in numerous local variations. The rights and obligations of *timar* holders differed from one part of the Empire to another. The history of Ottoman feudalism is usually divided into two periods: the period before the sixteenth century, during which the *timar-sipahi* system became fully developed, and the period after the sixteenth century, during which a new type of feudal lord appeared, the *chiftlik sahibi.*

Most historians think that in the first period Ottoman feudalism facilitated social progress and that in the second period it obstructed it. They explain that before the sixteenth century the relative peace (*Pax Ottomanica*), the moderate feudal obligations, and the stable and centralized Ottoman state organization stimulated prosperity. This stood in sharp contrast to the anarchy that prevailed in the Balkans before the Ottoman conquest. The absence of major disturbances among peasants is cited as proof that the people were relatively well off. After the sixteenth century, it is argued, Ottoman feudalism degenerated into an oppressive and unbearable institution, and there was, as a result, widespread social discontent and general stagnation.

A good many nationalists and Marxists argue that Ottoman feudalism was from the very start a primitive system and more backward than that of several of the conquered peoples. They reason that, despite the fact that it initially brought economic relief to the conquered peoples, the Ottoman feudalism was not as advanced as the feudalisms it superseded. It stifled progress, discouraged the development of productive forces, and produced a general social and economic setback. Muslim exclusiveness and the theocratic character of the Ottoman state, the destruction of material and human resources as a result of the Ottoman conquest, and the Ottoman state's relatively primitive technology and education are, in the opinion of Marxist authors, further explanations for its backwardness.

Transformation of Ottoman Feudalism. After the sixteenth century the administration of far-flung territories imposed heavy drains on the imperial treasury. Coupled with military defeats and territorial losses, this financial strain caused an economic crisis in the Ottoman Empire. Peasant disturbances and disorders became more frequent. For a state whose economy was based on war, military defeats precipitated a chain reaction that undermined the entire system. In order to have a more reliable and disciplined army, it became necessary to pay troops with money rather than with landed fiefs.

To obtain the funds required and to alleviate the general financial crisis, a decree in 1692 established a system of life farms (*malikane*) "for tax contracts in its grant." The new type of farms were virtually private property; with government approval they could be bought, sold, and willed to heirs. In return for the grant all that was expected was payment of a nominal fee to the State Treasury. Because tax-farmers had a life interest in their contracts, they found it expedient to collect fixed taxes and not to impose heavy burdens on the peasants. The system did not prove a satisfactory substitute for the previous *sipâhî* landownership, which, despite its shortcomings, was generally "paternal."

The difference between a landed fief (*timar*), a life farm (*malikane*), and a tax farm (*iltizam*), which the beneficiary (*multezim*) originally held for a year, even-

tually disappeared. In each case the relationship between
the landowner and peasant remained essentially the same.
The holders ultimately came into full possession of the
estates from which they collected taxes. The *timar-sipahi*
arrangement gradually broke down. The fief holders
began to ignore their military obligations and by various
irregularities were able to convert their fiefs into permanent holdings (*chiftliks*). Many of them turned villages
which had been deserted because of epidemics and wars
into private possessions. Janissaries and state officials
began to appropriate landed estates through purchase or
outright seizure. They acquired the peasants' lands and
tenants' rights in various ways. Thus many a peasant
acquired, besides his legal landlord who usually lived in
the city, another landlord (*chiftlik sahibi* or *beg*) who
established himself in the village. Rent and taxes were
paid to both. Under the new system the peasant continued to cultivate the land, but lost his right of tenantry
(*tasarruf*). As time passed much of the state (*miri*) land
was transformed into privately owned land (*mulk*).

The Chiftlik Sahibi. The new lord, or *chiftlik
sahibi,* was better able to protect the peasants and to
prevent his own rivals form raiding his manor, kid-
napping men, women, and children, and robbing him of
cattle and water. The new type of feudalism, according
to Stoianovich, had a tendency to spur the market
economy and to contribute to "the wider diffusion of
garden cultivation and of an irrigation or hydraulic
economy, including the more widespread planting of
rice and cotton and the introduction of a new crop,
maize." But the *chiftlik sahibi* imposed heavy burdens on
the peasants who became tenant farmers (*chiftchi*) at
best and serfs at worst. He took the largest share of the
harvest and demanded an increasing number of days of
free labor.

The *chiftlik sahibi* held his estate as fully inheritable
property and ignored any obligations that he might have
toward the state. In many cases he denied the peasants
the rights of usufruct and tenancy. In some areas peasants who had come to regard the houses in which they
lived and the land immediately adjacent as their immuta-
ble patrimony, even though subject to obligations toward

their feudal lords, were completely dispossessed. He had to give a tenth of his harvest to the "legal" fief-holder and to share the rest with the *chiftchi sahibi*. In many instances the peasant became completely dependent upon the new landlord. The result was increased peasant rebelliousness, mounting banditry, and the accelerated decline of the Empire. Personal security and economic pressure drove many peasants to cities, and there, unable to find employment, they banded together and resorted to mob violence and plundering forays into the countryside.

Nineteenth-Century Reforms. As the number of paid troops increased and the financial needs of the military grew, it became necessary to cancel fiefs granted to holders (*sipahis*) who no longer rendered military service and to transfer them to tax farmers (*iltizam*) with certain financial arrangements. In 1831, five years after the feudal cavalry had been dissolved and most of the fief-holders pensioned off, the *timar* system was abolished. Those of the feudal cavalry who had particular ability were reorganized into four squadrons of modern cavalry. Many fief-holders were also absorbed into the newly established provincial police system as salaried policemen or gendarmes.

The remnants of Ottoman feudalism lingered on, with the influence of the former *sipahis* remaining substantial. While the cancellation of *timars* appeared to assure large revenues to the state, it could not collect them. The situation was no better with regard to the lands held by religious endowments. Many a person who turned over his land to an endowment (*vakf*) took precautions to safeguard his ownership. The officials in charge of endowments (*mütevellis*), who came from the *ulema*, were as corrupt as other Ottoman agents. To impose firmer control over the religious endowments and to eliminate abuses in their administration, Mahmud II established a Directorate of *Vakf* (*Evkaf*), which later became a ministry. The Directorate collected revenues from the endowments, paid the costs of their administration, and transmitted the remainder of the proceeds to the imperial Treasury.

At least two important laws concerning land tenure were issued in the nineteenth century. The Land Law of

1858 prohibited the acquisition of whole villages as private estates. As many individuals had bought such properties in view of the growing volume of agricultural exports, the government tried to discourage the increase of large landed domains. The laws were not enforced, and the number of powerful freeholding *aghas* rose, with the peasants becoming either paid laborers or share-croppers. The peasant was thus no better off than he had been before; he paid taxes to the state, shared his harvest with the landlord, and performed free labor for him.

The second law, establishing land tenure relations which remained in force until the Ottoman Empire collapsed, was the Safer decree of 1859 codifying the existing rules regarding the obligations and rights of the serfs and the rights of the landlords. The rights of the peasants were attested to by a contract, and the peasants were obliged to pay in return a tithe (*hak*), which was precisely regulated (usually one third of the income remaining after a tenth for the tax had been subtracted). The landlord was required to provide his serfs with housing and could not evict them from the estate so long as they paid the tithe and worked the land satisfactorily. Serfs themselves could leave their landlords. In other words, the landlord was limited in his possession of the estate, and the peasant's tenant rights were guaranteed so long as he met his obligations.

6

SOCIAL INTERACTION, MOBILITY, AND ISOLATION

Much of the confusion in interpreting Ottoman social history has derived from excessive reliance upon Ottoman laws and Islamic theories. The result tends to confound the ideal of the Empire with the real.

Social Differentiation. The Ottoman population may be divided along religious lines into the favored Muslims and the tolerated scriptuarians; along occupational lines into the rural and urban population; and along social and economic lines into the upper and the lower classes. Stoianovich divides it into four estates (*ulema*—Men of the Pen; *asker*—Military class; *tüccar* —merchants or craftsmen; *rayah*—the subjects, flock, people, cattle).

Actually the Ottoman population was made up of the ruling class of Muslims who professed loyalty to the Sultan and who followed Ottoman customs, and the subject class or *rayah,* made up of those who lacked either one or both of these characteristics. Each of the two classes had its functions and privileges, the first governing and defending the Empire and exploiting the imperial wealth while the second produced this wealth. Each class consisted of different social groups (*sinif*).

The Village versus the City. In the European part of the Empire the ruling Turks lived in the cities and subject Christians in villages. For the subjects the city was the home of the oppressor, the tax-collector, and the policeman, while the village was the home of the oppressed and exploited peasant, taxpayer, and food-producer. In the Muslim regions, such as the Arab countries, the difference between the rural and the urban population was not ethnic, but social and economic. The well-to-do feudatories and the ruling elements lived in cities and the peasants in villages. The separation of village from city in all parts of the Empire produced a dichotomy of mores, habits, and customs, which in time developed into a struggle between two ways of life. The unbridged chasm between city and village is still one of the major problems in the Near East.

The peasants and nomads represented the largest social class in the Ottoman Empire. In the Balkans the peasants were the real representatives of the Greek, Bulgarian, and Serbian nations. The national liberation of these peoples was the achievement of the villages, which, in the words of Finlay, nourished "sentiments of manly vigor and true patriotism." The peasants were the mainstay of the insurrectionary movements against Turkish rule. It was the village that perpetuated the national tradition and preserved the ethnic individuality of each people. As a rule, Christian peasants were the most oppressed element of the population.

The Ottomans repopulated, renovated, and enlarged the old cities in Anatolia and the Balkans and built new ones. While the earlier period of Turkish rule witnessed the Turkification of the conquered cities, the final period in the Balkans, especially after the eighteenth century, witnessed their de-Turkification. The emigration of Muslims to Turkey and the influx of Christian peasants into the cities profoundly altered the ethnic and social structure. The Anatolian cities retained their Turkish complexion, and the Arab cities never lost their Arab character.

In nearly all cities the Christians, Jews, and Gypsies (who paid a special tax) lived in their own quarters (sing. *mahalle*). While the Muslims predominated in the cities of Bulgaria and Yugoslavia until the eighteenth century, the Christians living in them were largely Greeks, Armenians, and Tsintsars rather than Bulgars and Serbs. The Jews and foreigners such as Ragusans and Germans also lived in these cities. The city dwellers engaged in buying and selling; they were as merchants, artisans, or money-lenders.

Privileged Classes. There was a surprising degree of vertical mobility in Ottoman society. A Christian could become rich and a Muslim poor. By adopting Islam, one could raise his position on the social scale from that of a tolerated scriptuarian to that of a favored Muslim. Although the Empire had no hereditary aristocracy, apart from the dynasty itself, it did have privileged classes. The government and palace officials, commanders of the armed forces, and feudal landlords constituted the upper class, for example. Muslim teachers and jurists who led the public prayers, taught religion, interpreted the *Sheria,* and guarded Islamic tradition functioned as a sort of clergy and as such constituted a privileged class.

The Christian subjects had their own rich class. The nobles who adopted Islam or collaborated with the Turks were allowed to retain their estates. In the fifteenth century a few Christian *sipahis* did military service in exchange for land grants. Other privileged Christian groups were either created by the Ottoman rulers or developed through the acquisition of wealth. Among them were the Greek *archontes* who constituted a kind of official aristocracy which administered its own affairs, lived well, and acted as agents of Turkish dignitaries. There were also *phanariots,* patrician Greek families from the Phanar district of Istanbul, who supplied prominent government functionaries, and the Rumanian *hospodars.* The *phanariots* were sometimes called the "Christian Turks," a term which seems to describe aptly their moral and political position. In the Christian upper class one should also include the *amira* (the wealthy Armenian urban class) and the higher Christian clergy (patriarchs, bishops, and metropolitans).

Despite established electoral procedures, simony was widespread in the Christian communities. Especially after the sixteenth century, the higher Christian clergy bought their sees just as the Turkish pashas bought their posts, and, like the pashas, they obliged the people to pay back what they spent. Finlay found the higher Christian clergy opportunistic and ready "to sacrifice the interests of their nation" to achieve material gain and satisfy personal ambitions. Enjoying a substantial revenue from taxes and large monasterial properties, the higher clergy lived well. Their power was not confined to spiritual matters, but extended also into political life.

Tribal leaders, both Muslim and non-Muslim, in various parts of the Empire received special rights and privileges in exchange for their subservience. Whether elected, hereditary, or appointed, the elders (sing. *knez*) of the Serbian community or village and the Greek *khojabashi* were sometimes set apart from the ordinary *rayah*. Other privileged Christians were those who served as military auxiliaries or guards, cared for horses and provisions, and engaged in reconnoitering work and police duties. They were paid, granted lands, and exempted from feudal obligations.

Among the Muslims, local religious teachers and judges had much less economic potential and personal prestige than those of provincial or higher rank. The same was true of the lower Christian clergy. The monastic community, from which came the bishops and patriarchs, constituted the clerical upper class, while the secular clergy, who served in the parishes and often shared the common lot, made up the lower class. Finlay tells us that the secular clergy, although they lacked learning and possessed little power, exercised through their close relations with the peasantry an influence over the fate of their nation "quite incommensurate with their social rank." They supplied some of the "moral strength" which enabled the Greeks, Serbs, Bulgars, and others to resist Ottoman power.

Shifts in Population. Frequent wars, epidemics, and insurrections caused large shifts of population and significant demographic changes in the Empire. From the very beginning the Turks adopted a policy of sedentarization, by which nomadic and semi-nomadic peoples were settled as agriculturists or military auxiliaries (as was the case with the Vlachs). This method of settlement and colonization, called *sürgün,* was sometimes dictated by penal and sometimes by political, economic, and military considerations. The Turks occasionally settled populations such as the Serbs along the Venetian and

Austrian frontiers and organized them into military units. There were translocations of peoples from Asia to the Balkans (Turkomans, Cherkess, etc.), from the Balkans to Asia Minor, and from one part of the Balkans to another. Istanbul attracted people from all corners of the Empire. Sometimes refugees from abroad sought asylum, such as the Jews of Spain and Portugal and the small colonies of Poles, Russians, Hungarians, and Tartars who at different times settled in the Ottoman Empire.

Many Greeks, Albanians, and Yugoslavs also emigrated to Italy, Venice, and Turkey. On several occasions Austrian authorities invited the Serbs to settle on their side of the frontier and enlisted them into the frontier army. In fear of retribution Serbs at different times fled to Austria. Of great significance were the mass migrations in the late 1690's and again in 1739 to Hungary and Austria, as a result of which the Serbs abandoned a large part of their original Balkan home, allowing Muslim Albanians to occupy it. The Albanian emigrations to Southern Italy and Sicily, to Dalmatia, and to Southern Hungary are likewise an important chapter in the ethnic history of the Balkans under the Turks. After the Turkish conquest of Constantinople, the Greek population appears to have declined in numbers. Moreover, the translocation of inhabitants brought about substantial changes in the ethnography of Greece. Under Turkish pressure, the Greek rural population abandoned sizable areas to the Albanians, who colonized the whole of Boeotia, Attica, Megaris, and several other districts. Large sections of Thrace, Macedonia, and Thessaly were settled by *yürüks* (nomad Turkomans) or granted to Turks from Asia Minor. The coasts of Greece were virtually depopulated as a result of Ottoman measures against the Greeks who collaborated with their Christian enemies. Greeks emigrated to Apulia, Corsica, and other parts of Europe. The scrambling of the population in the Ottoman Empire contributed toward a fusion of peoples of different ethnic and cultural backgrounds.

The Origin of New Ethnic Groups, and Ethnic Transformation. The ethnogenesis of peoples and the formation of tribes out of different ethnic and social groups belong to a not yet fully told chapter of Near

Eastern history. The existence of tribes such as those which were partly Montenegrin and partly Albanian, or those divided into families of which some profess Christianity and others Islam, suggests the complexity of Ottoman society. In Greece, the Islamization of indigenous elements was slight, and the Muslim population derived primarily from Turkish and Albanian colonization. In Bulgaria and Yugoslavia (particularly in Macedonia and Bosnia), both the Islamization of Slavs and the colonization of Turks were extensive.

A few smaller groups, such as the *Dönme* (members of the Sabatayan sect of the Jews), also went over to Islam. The settlement of Spanish Jews in Turkish cities in the fifteenth century and the conversion of some of them to Islam produced a highly competitive element which took over branches of trade and industry hitherto a Greek monopoly. The Jews became physicians, bankers, and merchants, and many of them occupied high social positions.

Social Organization. The Ottoman conquest abruptly halted the political and social development of the subject peoples, who sought security by trying to breathe new life into their own fading patriarchal institutions. In many parts of the Empire the Ottoman system provided conditions favorable to the preservation of the old social order, which in the medieval Balkans, for example, had begun to yield before the onslaught of state organization. The Ottoman conquest led to the regeneration of such patriarchal institutions as the tribe, the clan, and the pastoral community (*katun*). Ottoman rule encouraged joint-family living as a means of personal and economic security. The much discussed *zadruga* was the predominant social organization in certain parts of the Balkans. We do not know enough, however, about family life— dress, food, habits, health, housing, and furnishings—in the Ottoman Empire. It is impossible to corroborate reports that after the Ottoman conquest Balkan families increased and Muslim families shrank in size. The Turks might have wished to weaken local territorial and kinship organizations, but found it necessary to permit them as a means by which order could be maintained through application of the principle of collective responsibility.

National life in many instances came to center around "small tribal cells" protected by the Church. The Serbian self-governing community (*knežina*), and probably also the Greek "free communities" (*eleutherochória*), were not only tolerated by the Ottoman authorities, but integrated into the imperial administrative system—without, however, encouraging social intercourse between them and other communities in the Empire.

The Millet. After the conquest of Constantinople (1453) the Greek Orthodox Church was organized into a *millet* (community) under the Ecumenical Patriarch, located in Constantinople. While the Patriarch was considered by the Porte as the head of the *millet,* in reality the Orthodox Churches were administered by an "oligarchy of patriarchs" (those of Constantinople, Antioch, Alexandria, and Jerusalem), each of whom had complete control over affairs in his domain.

Other confessional groups were similarly constituted. The Muslims made up a Muslim *millet,* be they Turks, Arabs, or Kurds. The Gregorian Armenians (those of the national church) and several other denominations which did not accept the Chalcedonian doctrine were recognized as a *millet* in 1461. Because the Catholicos of Echmiadzin (the real head of the Gregorian Armenians) lived abroad, the Turks accorded the Armenian Patriarch in Constantinople the privileges which the Greek Orthodox Patriarch received. Nominally, the Armenian Patriarch was in charge of all denominations under his jurisdiction; in reality, each denomination had its own religious head. The Armenian community was referred to as the *millet-i sadika* (the loyal community) until the nineteenth century, and was not encumbered with the *devshirme*. Such conscription was applied only to the Greek Orthodox *millet*.

The Jewish *millet* was recognized in the fifteenth century and represented all four divisions of Jews (Rabbanites, Karaites, Ashkenazim, and Sephardim). The Catholic community was not formally recognized as a *millet* because many of its members were treated as "foreigners."

The institution of *millets* was dictated by expediency and in accordance with earlier Islamic experience. The

millet did not embrace a unified territory, or a homogeneous ethnic group, or peoples enjoying the same political
and juridical status. It consisted of communities isolated
from each other, enjoying different social, political, and
economic privileges and weakly linked through an ecclesiastical administration. Except for the urban clergy
and a few non-Muslims in major cities, the non-Muslims
of the rural regions had practically no contact with cities
and the outside world. The *millet* system—"the classic
way by which Islam tried to solve its minority problem"
—in the long run spelled the ruination of the empire.

In time, according to R. Davison, the system of *millet*
administration was sapped by "venality in the ecclesiastical hierarchies." The upper clergy, often in league with
Ottoman officials, bled the people financially. Moreover,
the *millets* offered "convenient opportunity" to the great
powers for intrigue among the minorities. The *millets*
made it possible for the seeds of nationalism to take root
more easily among the Sultan's subjects, thereby fostering separatist and divisive forces in the empire. It was,
therefore, essential to introduce changes in the *millet*
system.

The Porte had hoped that by weakening the control
of the clergy, peace and stability might be attained
through elimination of tyranny, corruption, and feuding.
Thanks to enlightened leadership, the Armenians were
quicker in introducing reforms than were the Greeks.
After much discussion new constitutions were confirmed
for the Greek Orthodox (1862), Armenian Gregorian
(1863), and Jewish *millets* (1865). The main feature of
these organic laws was the broadening of the principle
of popular representation, thereby increasing lay influence in the management of the *millet's* affairs. The Patriarchs retained their position under the new system as
civil heads of their respective *millets* and supreme spiritual heads, and so did the *hahambashi* (grand rabbi).

From the Ottoman standpoint the *millets* were a failure. The main reason was that they continued to empha-
size the religious and ethnic separateness of individual
Ottoman peoples instead of fostering *Osmanlilik,* the
political cry of the Tanzimat reformers.

The Greek Orthodox Church. The most important non-Muslim institution in the Ottoman Empire was the Greek Orthodox Church. Since the political power once vested in Christian temporal rulers was gone, the Church assumed some of the Emperor's prerogatives. The Church conserved the cultural heritage and tradition of its people and kept memories of the good old days fresh in the minds of its believers; in this way it helped preserve their ethnic individuality. The parishes and dioceses of the Orthodox ecclesiastical administration brought together peoples who were otherwise divided by geographical and social barriers.

Thus the Church fulfilled important functions in the community. It represented its followers before the Ottoman authority and upon occasion led them into rebellion against that authority. The Church kept in touch with the outside world (the Papacy, Venice, Austria, and Russia) and facilitated the passage of a small amount of European influence into the Ottoman realm. Above all else, the Church was the center of social life. There the people, dressed in their native garb, gathered on holidays and festive occasions, met to decide major questions, and sang their songs and did their simple dances.

The Orthodox Church was an instrument of the Ottoman state, and the relations between the two were in some regards analogous to the relations between church and state in Communist countries today. The state tolerated the church so long as it served as an auxiliary of its power. The Patriarch, elected by the synod of higher clergy, was confirmed by the Sultan, and he was ceremoniously installed. He enjoyed many rights, including his own court and prison and almost absolute jurisdiction over the followers of his church. His office ranked with that of a pasha of three horsetails.

Sometimes for political and sometimes for other reasons, the Turks permitted the Christians to create autocephalous ecclesiastical administrations. The Serbian Patriarchate of Peć, for instance, was restored in 1557 and then abolished once more in 1776. The animosity between the Orthodox and Latin churches, one good reason for the fall of the Byzantine state, continued after the Ottoman conquest. There were many instances of Orthodox persecution of Catholics and of the Sultan's

intervention on their behalf. The Porte defended its
"native" *zimmis* from Catholic encroachment and prose-
lytism. The prevailing situation often enabled the Porte
to play the churches against each other, to exact heavy
payments from the patriarchs and other religious dignitaries, and to banish, dismiss, and even execute the
leading clergy. At times the congregations were deci-
mated, churches desecrated, and the rights of religious
autonomy curtailed. When conditions became intolerable,
there were instances of discussion between high religious
spokesmen aimed at the union of the Orthodox and Latin
churches, and the clergy often led peasants into rebellion
against the Turks. Treasonable action by Church leaders
was vigorously prosecuted.

The long period of imposed restrictions and close association with the Ottoman government, however, had
negative effects on the development of the Orthodox
Church. Once a source of spiritual strength and intellectual power, the Church began to ossify. It was forced
to concern itself primarily with the physical preservation
of its members, to adjust to the needs of a patriarchal
society, and to tolerate much that was considered undesirable. Theology and learning declined to secondary
importance, and in these respects the Church stagnated
and has never recovered from the spiritual setback caused
by long Ottoman rule.

The Guilds. One of the important Ottoman institutions was that of the guilds, or *esnafs*—the associations
of merchants and artisans. The main purpose of the
guilds was to afford protection to their members and to
aid them in times of need. The guilds were made up of
men engaged in the same trade or craft. Tightly organized, they had their own officials, initiation ritual, and
symbols. From the very start the guilds served as important auxiliaries of the state, supplying some of the
goods required by the armed forces and the palace. At
one time they were so powerful that they controlled city
life; between 1700 and 1851, the *esnafs* in Sarajevo
virtually transformed the city into an "*esnaf* republic."

Although some were interdenominational, the guilds
were generally organized on confessional lines. The
statute of the Muslim *esnafs* were confirmed by Ottoman

authorities and those of Christians by church elders. For example, the Patriarch of Constantinople confirmed the Greek *esnafs,* and the Patriarch of Peć the Serbian *esnafs.* The Muslims had a virtual monopoly of certain crafts, while others were open to the Christians. The value of the guilds as instruments of "social fusion" between Muslims and non-Muslims is often exaggerated. Likewise the importance of non-Muslim and mixed guilds as a means of social and economic advancement was not as great as sometimes believed, because the guilds were limited in number and local in character. Contacts between Muslims and non-Muslims were not extensive even in common guilds. The guilds were primarily located in cities and not in rural areas, in which the overwhelming majority of the people lived.

The effects of the division of the crafts into Muslim and Christian types, as well as the *esnaf* organizational and professional terminology, have survived long after the collapse of the Ottoman power. In many parts of the ·Balkans Christians still follow tradition by gravitating toward certain crafts while the Muslims predominate in others. In the Communist countries, however, the last vestiges of the Ottoman guilds are rapidly disappearing.

Discrimination. The Ottoman state system fostered denominational and social discrimination, for the population was grouped by religions, classes, and ranks. One alleged purpose of this division was to separate various groups from one another "as much as possible in order to prevent contact and possible conflict." Each individual, in the words of S. Shaw, had a place in life established by his social status, and within "the bounds (*hadd*) of his place, he was absolute." Consequently, the Ottoman possessions in Europe were never assimilated "either to Islam or to the Turkish language," and in the Balkans, writes B. Lewis, the peasant masses "remained Christian, alien in language and culture as well as in religion, outside the cultural horizon of the 'Turks.'" The confessional and social compartmentalization was scarcely adopted by the Ottoman rulers out of altruistic reasons, but rather in order to make it easier for them to rule the heterogeneous populations they had conquered.

The non-Muslims were never able to mix freely in

Muslim society. As subject infidels they were socially
castigated and denied many of the rights enjoyed by
the ruling Muslims. The government was Muslim, and
the official language was Turkish. It was Islam and not
the Turkish "national identity" that separated the rulers
from the ruled. The Turks thought of themselves "almost exclusively as Muslims," and in this way they were
no different from many of their subjects. Not until the
nineteenth century did the concepts of "a Turkish nationality" and "Ottomanism" develop. But as already
indicated, not all Muslims were held equal. After the
seventeenth century we note, for example, a tendency
for the "born" Muslims to blame "converted" Muslims
for the empire's plight.

There was also a class discrimination. The titled and
well-to-do in the Ottoman Empire were honored, and
the lower classes were looked down upon. The term
rayah was not applied to non-Muslim subjects alone, but
to lower Muslim social classes as well. In localities
where there were no Christians, the lowest social class
was the Muslim *rayah*. But while the Muslim *rayah* was
economically oppressed and socially discriminated against
just as much as the Christian *rayah,* the latter were also
legally and religiously discriminated against. A distinction was made between the *rayah* of the ruling faith
and the *rayah* of the subject nation. Some non-Muslim
rayah occasionally procured "special agreements" which
gave them economic favors not available to the Muslim
rayah, but such privileges were exceptional. So sharp
was the line between the *rayah* and the rest of the population that as time passed, the *rayah* developed its own
mores and way of life.

The Poll Tax. Payment of a poll tax (*jizye*) by
Christians in lieu of military service has been variously
interpreted. Did it represent discrimination against the
non-Muslims, or did it not? According to Islamic practice
only the Muslims, as true believers, were eligible to fight
for the faith. This rule, however, was not always adhered to.

To placate the national demands of the various subject
peoples, the Ottoman government abolished the "duty
and privilege of military service" in 1855. Lewis tells
us that the Christians "were even less anxious to accept

the privilege of arms than were the Muslims to confer
it." Under the new system Christians could hold only
the lower ranks and were subjected to many restrictions.
While Christians, when their national interests inter-
vened, served on occasion in the Ottoman army (e.g.,
Armenians in the Russo-Turkish War of 1877-1878),
as a general rule they avoided military service. For the
Christians to serve in the infidel army meant fighting
against the Christian world with which they were in
sympathy.

Clothing. After the Ottoman conquest there was
a gradual "Turkification" of clothing in many parts of
the Empire. The dress worn by different Ottoman subjects, however, was not always a mere copy of Turkish
styles. Often it represented either a local adaptation of
that dress or an entirely indigenous creation. Nonetheless, the "Turkification" of clothing was extensive, and
a large Turkish or Persian or Arabic nomenclature enriched the vocabulary of many non-Turkish subjects.

Turkish influence on the clothing of the subject peoples
was the result of both voluntary imitation and official
regulations. The Turks did not like to see Christians
copy their clothing and forbade them to wear expensive
and brightly colored clothes as well as garments in the
"sacred" color of green. To a good Muslim, an acceptance of infidel headgear implied social degradation and
religious betrayal. The insistence on clothing that distinguished Muslim from non-Muslim encouraged similar
tendencies among the Christians. If in the nineteenth
century the Muslims made the *fez* a mark of their faith,
the Montenegrins did the same with their *zavrata*. Nonetheless, many a non-Turk had a suppressed desire to
dress like a Turk and to free himself of regulated clothing.
On occasion the Muslims and Christians clashed over the
clothing.

As Ottoman rule weakened and Christians gained a
greater degree of freedom, some Christians gradually
proceeded to copy the Turks in clothing and jewelry.
One of the first things the Serbs did after the liberation
in 1804 was to don Turkish dress—the fancier clothes
of their rulers. Later, as political and cultural contacts
with the West expanded, everything associated with the

Turks came to be regarded as backward and alien. In the course of the nineteenth and twentieth centuries the clothing of urban residents became rapidly Westernized just as, writes ˈSh. Mardin, the new Ottoman officials began "wearing cutaway coats and fezzes instead of the flowing robes and turbans." The process of Westernization was slower in villages, and until recently many villages have clung to traditional garb which betrays Ottoman influence.

Though by 1860 the condition of the Christians had improved, they continued to suffer from unequal treatment. R. Davison observes that "They still protested the general prohibition of bells on their churches, the frequent rejection of their testimony in Turkish courts, occasional rape of Christian girls or forced conversions, and other sorts of personal mistreatment."

7

OTTOMAN CULTURE

One critic writes that the Ottomans contributed nothing original to world culture and that "such graces of civilization as the Turk has acquired have practically all been taken from the subject peoples whom he so greatly despises." He notes that the writing and religion of the Turks were Arabic, their best literary style Persian, and their architecture Byzantine. The well-known French statesman, George Clemenceau, contends that wherever the Turkish rule was established there was "a fall in the level of culture." A popular Serbian saying states that "Where the Turkish horse trotted there the grass stopped growing!"

General Character of Ottoman Culture. Ottoman culture was basically a synthesis of the Central Asian and Anatolian (Hittite, Persian, Greek, Roman, Byzantine, etc.) heritage. Yet from early times the Turkish leaders were conscious of their ethnic individuality and made a distinction between the "Turkish element" and the "Arabo-Persian tendencies" in the Ottoman court. They used the Turkish language in their local administration and governed their daily lives according to Turkish customs. While they saw to it that Arabic and Persian classics of literature, theology, and science were translated into Turkish, they also sponsored the writing of and sometimes themselves wrote books on subjects taken from Turkish life, in a form different from the Persian model. Turkish epic poems and popular sagas and myths supplied inexhaustible literary material. The Ottoman writers and thinkers were of two kinds. One kind (*ulema-i rusum*) supported the existing system, idealized the es-

67

tablished order, and created the Ottoman ideology. The other kind (*khaiq-Ulemasi*) based their writings on tendencies derived from the people and on popular hopes and aspirations. But Ottoman culture was a class culture, a monopoly of the upper classes. A refined, educated, and learned person was referred to as an Osmanli, while an illiterate peasant of Asia Minor was given the appellation of Turk. The former was proficient in Persian and Arabic; the latter, who spoke the crude Turkish vernacular, was looked down on as a rough Turk (*Kaba Turk*) or donkey Turk (*Eshek Turk*). The word "Turk" was generally used "to denote the nomads or peasants of Anatolia," in much the same way as "fellah" is used in modern Arabic.

Inhibited by the Islamic tabu on the representation of living beings in art, the Ottoman Turks had little to show in the field of painting and sculpture, but in decorative arts they produced a style and form distinctly their own. One can refer to the exquisite writings and illumination of copies of the Koran, carvings on mosques and tombs, and ornaments in brass, copper, and silver. It would be stretching the point to attribute the beautiful miniature painting, tile decoration, wood and mother-of-pearl inlay, gold and silver embroidery, and tooled leather work produced in the Ottoman Empire exclusively to the Persian, Arab, and Armenian genius; such works incorporate a synthesis of a number of cultural influences, including Turkish.

Cultures of Ottoman Subjects. Ottoman rule had a devastating effect on the cultural life of most of the conquered nations. In the Balkans, for example, learning virtually dried up, and art deteriorated from the exquisite medieval masterpieces to simple primitive creations. Once on a cultural level with the rest of Europe, the Balkan peoples had fallen far behind by the nineteenth century. There were several reasons for this lag. The Ottoman regime obliterated many of the spiritual and material resources of the subject peoples. Medieval states were eradicated, scions of conquered nobility killed off, churches and monasteries demolished, lands devastated, settlements destroyed, and large segments of the population dispersed. The Christian communities, deprived of their own resources for development, were given no comparable substitute. Moreover, they were isolated from cities and the mainstream of civilization, and restricted primarily to rural and pastoral life.

As a result of long Turkish rule, the Balkan peoples became "the most backward" in Europe. Like the Turks themselves, they were by-passed by the Renaissance and the Reformation. When Humanism started to cast its rays over Western Europe, "darkness" descended over the Balkan lands that once again would have to undergo the metamorphosis from tribalism to nationhood.

The state did not provide for the enlightenment of the people of the non-Muslim *millets;* indeed, it discouraged almost every form of learning. While feudal landlords and state functionaries helped establish educational institutions for training the Muslim elite, the impoverished Christian communities depended largely on taxes and the contributions of their own people for the building of schools and churches. Greeks, Armenians, Tsintsars, and Jews who lived in the major cities were exposed to some learning; they could study abroad and could buy favors. Many of them served as *dragomans* (interpretors) or held prominent government positions.

The Greek *phanariots,* who had both the means and the privileges, demonstrated a certain amount of creative genius. To them, and to the prosperous Greek merchants and well-to-do expatriates, one must largely attribute the relatively high level of education that the Greeks achieved during the eighteenth and nineteenth centuries. The social uplifting in the Greek world came in spite of Ottoman rule rather than because of it. One must not ignore the importance of many monastery and church schools, the school of the Patriarchate, itinerant teachers, and the educational institutions in Syria and elsewhere founded by Catholic missionaries from the seventeenth century on and by the Protestant missionaries after the 1820's. But these efforts were outside the Ottoman system and were grossly inadequate.

What particularly impeded progress in the Ottoman Empire was Islamic exclusiveness, which hindered the exchange of ideas between regions and peoples. Yet the lives of most individuals and of many villages and other corporate units were not completely controlled by the State. The subjects were granted "a politically irrelevant form of self-government," which Wittfogel describes as "a Beggars' Democracy." The media of mass communication were designed "not to enlighten and persuade opinion, but to prepare and prescribe behavior." Public criers "were not used for official announcement to non-Muslims," but instead their heads were summoned "to receive the news on behalf of their constituencies."

The Anti-Literate Elite. Made up of "a variety of illiterate population," the Ottoman Empire, in the words of Daniel Lerner, was regulated by "an anti-literate elite." Far from being illiterate itself, this elite was jealous of its position and endeavored to monopolize education. It considered too much learning a threat to Islam and tradition. The Sultans were educated and knew Arabic and Persian besides their own Ottoman language. They patronized literature and the arts, founded libraries, and left properties to religious endowments which sustained schools and centers of learning. Nor were all the Sultans entirely immune to the influence of Christian civilization. Mehmed the Conqueror appreciated Greek works and had Greek writers and other foreigners on his palace staff. The Sultans often made use of Greeks in building their fleet and mosques. But all this was spasmodic and incidental. The Turks refused to print books because the "scriptures would no longer be scriptures if they were printed." The first press and paper factory did not appear in Turkey until 1728-1729, and Turkish journalism did not begin until 1861, when the first private paper was issued. Several subject peoples of the empire had printing presses before the sixteenth century. The result, according to Lerner, was that "independent rates of social change occurred . . . the Christians modernizing faster than others."

Medieval Literature. The Turks have always been partial to poetry, both folk and classical. In poetry they attained their highest literary art, and with the possible exception of the short story, poetry remains for them the most appreciated medium of literary expression. When talking about Ottoman literature, one must distinguish the thriving popular literature from the sophisti-

cated and restrictive classical literature. The folk literature embraces "a wealth of old Turanian ballads and
epics." The products of folk literature are tales (by
Dede Korkut, Ashik Kerem, and others), anecdotes,
legends, myths, narrations of the miraculous deeds of
the saints, proverbs, riddles, songs, ballads, epics, hymns,
the works of mystic poets and minstrels (Yunus Emre,
Kaygusuz, and others), and the humorous literature of
Nasreddin Hoja and Karagöz. The classical literature,
on the other hand, reached only a very small portion of
the Empire's population and had virtually no influence
on the non-Muslim communities. Most of the classical
authors were prominent state or religious leaders. Several
sultans were better-than-average poets. A substantial part
of the classical literature consisted of translations from
or adaptations of Persian, Arabic, and other Muslim
works, written in Persian or Arabic.

For a long time the leading Turkish authors wrote in
Persian, and in Persian form and meter. Their conception of poetry was also Persian. Earlier Turkish
simplicity was abandoned, and metaphors, similes, homo-
nyms, anagrams, and other kinds of rhetorical embellish-
ments were adopted. There is a great deal of repetition,
with the same phrases and clichés used over and over
again. The Persian emphasis on the exotic, and the Arab
emphasis on scholarship, were strongly manifested in
Ottoman cultural life. But the development of a classical
literature written in a foreign language and style widened
the breach between the peasantry and the ruling and
urban classes. The use of foreign languages and adherence to traditional classical form and content ham-
pered the growth of a distinctive Ottoman Turkish literature.

The Turks had great difficulty in establishing their
identity *vis-à-vis* Persian and Arabic influences. It took
a long time before the vernacular of Anatolia was eventually raised by poets, chroniclers, and others to the position of a language of culture and learning. *Divan**

* *Divan* is a mixture of Persian epic and religious mysticism,
combined with Arab Islamic thought and learning. Its
name is derived from the poetic form in which it was
usually published.

literature began appearing in the Turkish language at the beginning of the fourteenth century, following the example set by the poet Yunus Emre, who is still a powerful figure in Turkish folk poetry. While this type of literature continued to grow during the next four centuries, Persian forms, language, and mysticism remained substantial, and many writers still employed a heavily Persianized and Arabicized Turkish.

Both Fuzuli and Baki (*see Reading No. 8*) wrote in Turkish, which came into vogue at the courts of Selim I and Suleiman the Magnificient, the two great rulers of the sixteenth century. The court poets used the Anatolian dialect in composing *Turkis* and popular ballads. Gradually the Turkish classical language developed. The ethnic element of Ottoman literature nonetheless remained weak. Richard Robinson writes that only a few mediocre writers were moved by the idea of Turkism (*Türkcülük*), seeking without success to make the Turks "conscious of their common racial and cultural origins."

The Ottomans achieved their greatest prominence in courtly and religious literature in the eighteenth century. Nedim (1681-1730) initiated a new trend in Ottoman literature. He used a syllabic meter in a classical poem, and changed the subject matter from allegorical to descriptive, drawing inspiration from his own Istanbul environment. The second of the great eighteenth-century authors was Sheykh Ghalib (1757-1798), the last important poet to follow the *divan* tradition which after the eighteenth century was increasingly overshadowed by Westernizing influences.

The prose medium attained importance for the first time in the seventeenth century, with the appearance of the well known travelogues and histories by Katib Chelebi and Evliya Chelebi, various ambassadorial reports, pronouncements on domestic affairs prepared by the Sultans, and the records of court chroniclers. It was in this period that Naima (1655-1716) lifted Ottoman historiography to its highest point. The prose narrative did not come into its own until a century later.

Other than the folk *karagöz* (shadow play), *orta oyunu* (a form of improvised comedy with set plots), and the tales of the *meddah* (public story-teller), modern drama was unknown until after the middle of the nineteenth century. Of no small consequence was the development of the popular counterpart of the big-city theater, the so-called *tuluat* or improvised drama presented by roving companies of actors throughout anatolia.

Modern Literature. The eighteenth century witnessed significant development in Ottoman cultural and intellectual life, but the real beginnings of modern Ottoman literature did not come until the nineteenth century, when a number of foreign works were translated and a growing number of original works produced. Out of classical, folk, and Western literary movements there gradually evolved a new liberal and nationalistic Ottoman literary tradition. (See pp. 96 ff.)

New literature was initiated by Shinasi (1826-1871), the first Turk to write a modern drama, to found a private newspaper, and to treat political questions in poetry. Shinasi's "Marriage of a Poet" (*Sai Evlenmesi*), which appeared in 1860, was the first European-type play published in Turkey; it was also important because it openly advocated the liberation of women. Ziya Pasha (1825-1880) pleaded in favor of folk literature as the basis of a new Turkish literature. The most distinguished of the writers in this period was Namik Kemal (1840-1888), who espoused through his works the causes of constitutionalism.

The new Turkish literature, at the start largely imitative and based chiefly on French models, acquired originality by the twentieth century. At the same time that the new literature was being adopted, the tendency was to keep the old folk literature but discard the classical literature.

The end of the nineteenth century, particularly after the failure of the Young Turks in 1911, gave birth to a literary movement (*milli edebijat*) which aimed to Turkify and simplify the language of literature. The most prominent in the movement was Ziya Gökalp. He published a periodical called *Young Pens* (*Genj Kalemler*) in Salonika in 1911, and gave substance to modern Turkish political nationalism (*Türkiyechilik*), of which Mustafa Kemal Ataturk became the "Living embodiment."

The attempt in the wake of the Kemalist revolution to reject everything associated with the Ottoman civilization failed. In the contemporary Turkish literature and theater one sees the conflict between old and new and between East and West. The Turkish writers and artists continue to draw inspirations from the Ottoman tradition.

Art and Architecture. The Ottomans carried on the Anatolian heritage in art. The synthesizing of a manifold artistic heritage which began in the time of the Seljuks continued under the Ottomans. A discerning historian can detect Arabic and Persian elements in Ottoman art and architecture, as well as Armenian, Byzantine, and other influences. The Seljuk bequeathed to Ottoman architecture "the beautiful stamp of delicacy." The domed basilic type of mosque betrays an unmistakable Byzantine origin.

Early Turkish architecture is characterized by massive walls of huge blocks of stone, ogival buttressed gateways with curves and niches, and decorative ornaments of different designs framing gateways, doors, and windows. Marble carvings and beautiful tiles in blue and turquoise colors give Turkish architecture and art a distinctive character. Another quality is the strength in the triple arches that support the cupolas of the mosques and palaces. The imperial domain was dotted with castles, fortresses, monasteries (*tekkes*), mosques and medresses, caravanserais, bridges, tombs, bathhouses, and fountains built in exquisite taste and delicate style and form. (*See Reading No. 7.*)

The major mosques were enriched with carved gateways and pulpits and with brocades, silks, and carpets in shimmering colors. The famous mosques, such as Aya Sofia (the transformed Christian church of St. Sofia), those founded by the sultans Mehmed II, Selim I, Suleiman I, Bayazid II, and the ones built by humbler persons (Yeni Valideh Jami), are the finest examples of Ottoman artistic genius. Only minor alterations were needed to adapt Aya Sofia to the Islamic ritual. Magnificent gold mosaics were covered by limestone chalk. The *qiblah* (the direction of prayer toward Mecca) was designated by a niche called the *mihrab*. A *minbar* (pulpit) was installed, and four minarets (towers for the prayer callers, *muezzins*) were built. The converted church was surrounded by *türbe* (mausoleums), *medrese,* and reinforcements.

Among the outstanding Ottoman monuments one may cite the *Ulu Jami* in Brusa, built in the time of Orkhan and Murad I. It is an unadorned hall of columns of rectangular form, with five naves and four cupolas. Carl Brockelmann considers the mosque of Sultan Mehmed the Conqueror "the most perfect monument of Ottoman architecture." It was erected by the Greek architect Christodulos. The interior was cruciform, crowned by a vast central dome resting on four columns. Schools, baths, hospitals, and kitchens surrounded it. The mosque was virtually destroyed by an earthquake in 1767. Bayezid II built a mosque distinguished "by the opulence of material and the Persian style of decoration. Pointed arches of alternating black and white marble on costly pillars of jasper and *verde antico,* with elegant stalactite capitals." The Selimiye Mosque in Edirne was designed by the great architect Sinan. The Mosque of Suleiman the Magnificent, which Robert Michens describes in his book, has four minarets, beautiful windows, jeweled glass, delicate tiles on the wall surrounding the *mihrab,* and a chapel. Its internal proportions are deceptive combining massiveness with grace. The central dome is flanked by a number of small domes. In the foreground stands a fine fountain covered with a cupola. The roof of the cloisters is broken up into 24 little domes. Behind the mosque lies a garden in which are found the *türbe* (tombs) of Suleiman the Magnificent and his Roxelana, "the Joyous One." The mosque shows Byzantine influence in its basilica architecture, but the balconies and tall minarets are distinctly Islamic. The Mosque of Muhammad Ali in Cairo probably represents the finest example of Ottoman architecture outside Anatolia and the Balkans.

In some parts of Yugoslavia, Bulgaria, and Turkey, especially in the small communities, whole blocks of dwellings and small shops built in the Ottoman style during Ottoman rule are still standing. Large parts of Turkey and the Arab world abound with Ottoman architectural survivals. In Anatolia simple village huts and small village mosques remain almost as they were in Ottoman days. In many of the homes there is still an *oda* (room) to which men retire after sundown either for a meal or for the ritual prayer of Islam. One must distinguish, however, true Ottoman architecture from what may be merely Ottoman-influenced architecture, for, as already indicated, the Ottoman Empire was a mosaic of autochtonous cultures. Thus, for example, the Anatolian house and mosque exhibit a style and structural form very different from those in Syria, Iraq, and elsewhere.

The trend toward modernity has been progressively undermining Ottoman artistic and architectural influence. From the eighteenth century on while traditional art continued to thrive, there was an increasing tendency to recognize the importance of Western art. One detects Western influence in eighteenth-century Turkish architecture and decoration, and Westerners were called upon to paint portraits. This process had been speeded up by the rapid growth of urbanism in recent years. By the nineteenth century Western art and architecture had made permanent inroads, and the process was greatly accelerated in Kemalist Turkey. Ankara, with its block buildings, severely plain and modern, is a most un-Turkish-looking city. In the Balkans where Ottoman architectural influence was dominant at one time, the cities rapidly shed their oriental character and acquired a modern look. Today neither Sofia nor Athens nor Belgrade betrays any traces of Ottomanism.

Music. The musical heritage of Turkey consisted of Eastern music taken from Greeks via Byzantines—passed to Arabs and later to Persians and Ottomans—and folk music, which represented a continuation of ancient Turkish music. Monophonic and melancholic Turkish music has a plaintive and nostalgic ring. Doric, Eolic, and Phrygian modes frequently occur in it. The folk music is characterized by distinct lowering of pitch within each musical phrase.

Particularly significant is the Turkish popular song of love and heroism. One encounters in the lyrics constant references to death and frustrated love. Prominent in Ottoman musical tradition are the bards (*ozan, cogur, ashik*) who wandered about the country, singing and reciting poetry "in the popular rhythm and in traditional forms" to the accompaniment of the old Turkish string instrument called *kopuz*. Westerners find Turkish music more "a musical curiosity than music." Ronart describes it as "an ecstatic wrestling-match of voices, a duet of two individual melodic phrases executed with the most primitive of instruments, a breath-taking rush of cadences amid twirling tambourines."

The Turks and their subject peoples have a common musical heritage, and the uninitiated see little difference between Turkish music and say, that of the Greeks, Bulgars, and Arabs. The Orthodox, Armenian, Chaldean, and African churches as well as Jewish synagogues were also the heirs of Eastern music. Hence this same musical heritage was common to all Ottoman subjects. Yet in time each of the many Ottoman subject nations developed its own distinctive music. While they did not sing each other's songs, they did influence each other's music. Like the Turkish bard who sang to the accompaniment of the *kopuz,* the Serbian *guslar* chants and narrates his epic songs to the accompaniment of the primitive *gusle,* a stringed instrument which came to him from Asia Minor, probably in the eleventh century.

Perhaps no Balkan song is more beautiful and rich in Oriental flavor than the *sèvdalinka* (*sèvdàh*—Arabic for "love" and "desire of love") of Bosnia or the *dèrtliska* (*dèrtli*—Persian and Turkish for "worry" and "grief") of Macedonia. The very popular *sèvdalinka* is the expression of a man's and woman's emotions, combining sentimentalism and oriental passion. The melancholy *dèrtliska* tells of one's concern about life and love, sadness and pain. One of the most interesting aspects of musical trends is that the folk music of the Near Eastern peoples has retained its popularity, despite the invasion of modern music.

— 8 —

THE OTTOMAN EMPIRE IN DECLINE: EIGHTEENTH AND NINETEENTH CENTURIES

The geographic, administrative, and legal diversity and social and economic disparity, the government based on Muslim religious exclusiveness and principles of theocracy, and the isolation of ethnic and confessional entities from the main streams of civilization account for a ramshackle empire doomed to crumble. (*See Reading No. 11.*) Apart from some success in stirring loyalty to the Sultan as a symbol of state, the Ottoman Empire failed to develop the sense of belonging in the minds of its subjects. That it lasted as long as it did can be attributed to the international situation, to a few good sultans and dedicated grand vezirs, and to many whose well-being was inextricably linked to the Ottoman system.

In retrospect, one can discern signs of decline in the time of Suleiman the Magnificent. After the latter's death the decline became more apparent. Weak sultans succeeded one another, and the Empire suffered major military and naval defeats. No fewer than 13 sultans ruled between 1566 and 1718, of whom only two (Murad IV, 1623-1640, and Mustafa II, 1695-1703) showed signs of ability. One sultan was murdered and three dethroned. Selim II (1566-1574) was a drunkard, and his son Murad III (1574-1595) strangled five brothers, spent twenty years with his harem, and produced 103 children. Mehmed III (1595-1603) did away with 19 brothers. Such was the general trend toward anarchy that characterized the central government. Not until the emergence in 1656 of the Köprülü dynasty of grand vezirs was an unsuccessful attempt made to reform the empire.

Palace intrigues, instigated by women and eunuchs of the harem, and widespread government corruption betrayed political and economic instability. Social insurrections in which both Muslims and Christians particpated became more frequent. The institutional system started to disintegrate, and officials began to encroach on each other's spheres of activity. The *timar-sipahi* relations— the basis of Ottoman feudalism—broke down, and exploitation of the peasantry was intensified. It has been popular in some circles to attribute the decline of the Ottoman Empire to its betrayal by converts who by the seventeenth century had allegedly established a stranglehold on the government. This explanation ignores many basic problems.

Until the middle of the sixteenth century imperial revenues derived from taxes and other sources were sufficient to maintain the government and the military establishment. The Sultan himself was able to finance his costly palace out of his huge income from imperial lands, mines, salt, autonomous provinces, trade, and customs duties. In 1564 for the first time the government experienced a financial deficit, which occurred regularly from then on. The Sultans often met deficits by debasement of the currency.

Successive monetary crises, high prices of bread and other commodities, the importation of cheap Western silver and currency, and a decline in wages contributed to the plight of the Empire. At the same time the marked price increases on Turkish goods and smaller increases on imported goods, along with a great volume of foreign trade in the seventeenth century, stimulated commerce in Ottoman towns and villages and fostered the growth of a market economy. Crafts and trade expanded, and guilds increased in number and productivity. But the result was not a social and economic revolution such as took place in the West. Commercial life on a considerable scale was restricted to a few major cities, and a primitive economy continued to prevail in the vast areas of the Empire. Social change proceeded at an extremely slow tempo.

Military Setbacks. In 1570 the Ottoman demands for the surrender of Cyprus forced Venice to appeal to Pope Pius V for help. The Pope responded with financial aid and an appeal to Christian princes and the Persian Shah. Philip II of Spain, Cosmo dei Medici (Duke of Tuscany), and a number of Italian states joined in a Holy League against the Turks. The allied fleet, commanded by Don Juan of Austria, crushed the Turkish navy at Lepanto in 1571. After celebrating this splendid victory, which showed that Turks were not invincible, the Christians dissolved their alliance. The Turks rebuilt their navy, regained control of the sea, and forced Venice to surrender Cyprus and to pay a war indemnity and tribute for some of its island possessions.

The defeat at Lepanto exposed the weakness of the Ottoman Empire as a maritime power. The war with Austria which was ended by the Treaty of Sitvatorok in 1606 similarly revealed the Empire's military decline; the treaty released Austria from the annual tribute which she had been paying to the Sultan. For the first time the Turks were forced to treat a European ruler on an equal footing rather than with contempt.

Despite these reverses and the frequent wars with Safavid Persia which forced the Empire to fight on two fronts, the Ottomans long remained a formidable military power and occasionally demonstrated real strength. In 1672 they captured Podolia from Poland and in 1683 sent a large army against Vienna. Impressive though the Turkish military power was, it suffered a defeat at the hands of King Jan Sobieski and the Polish and German troops defending the city.

The disaster at Vienna marked the beginning of the decline of the Ottoman Empire. Turkish expansion was stopped. From then on the Ottomans lost territory in nearly every major war. They ceased waging offensive wars and concentrated on the defense of their territories. Encouraged by their victory at Vienna, the Christian powers formed a Holy League and inflicted further defeats upon the Turks. By the Treaty of Carlowitz (1699) the Ottoman Empire lost all of Hungary to Austria, Podolia to Poland, Morea to Venice, and Azov to Russia. The Ottoman Empire, however, recovered somewhat and a few years later defeated the Russians, forcing them to return Azov by the Treaty of Pruth (1711). In the war of 1715-1718 the Turks were forced to surrender Serbia to Austria, but at the same time they expelled Venice from Morea and the islands of the Archipelago.

One important development at this time that greatly affected the future of the Ottoman Empire was the ascendancy of Russia. The first offical contacts between Russia and Turkey occurred in 1492, at the time when Grand Duke Ivan III ascended the Russian throne. Having married Sofia, niece of the Byzantine Emperor, Ivan conducted himself as successor to the last Byzantine dynasty, whose emblem, the two-headed eagle, he adopted. Not until the time of Tsar Ivan IV, "the Terrible" (1533-1584), did Russia and Turkey come into open conflict over possession of the northern approaches to the Black Sea and the Caucasus. It was then that Mehmed Sokolli, the grand vezir, contemplated building a canal between the Don and the Volga for the purpose of outflanking Persia and checking the Russian advance. In the latter part of the sixteenth century and in the following century Russia and Turkey were frequently involved in disputes and armed skirmishes, being drawn into the perpetual border strife between the Cossacks and the Tartars. From the time of Peter the Great (1682-1722) until the nineteenth century Russia and Austria fought the Turks together, after which the Russians alone made war against the Turks. Except for the wars fought in 1711 and in 1853-1856 (the Crimean War) the Turks were defeated by the Russians in six encounters.*

The crippling monetary burden of constant wars caused a financial drain which aggravated the already poor economic situation in Turkey. The Porte, to improve its military posture, attempted to introduce modern artillery, but this required resources which the lagging economy could not supply. The Empire failed to modernize and to equip properly its armed forces, nor was it in a position to pay the Janissaries and standing troops. Measures such as the sale of government offices undertaken to raise money only served to increase corruption

* The wars of 1735-1739, 1768-1774, 1778-1792, 1806-1812, 1827-1829, and 1877-1878.

and government chaos. Capitulations were granted to a growing number of foreign powers.

Insurrections. After the end of the sixteenth century the Ottoman Empire was beset by frequent internal uprisings,* inspired by conditions at home and abroad. The weaker the central power, the more intensive the resistance movements. If the Christians rebelled for religious rights and social justice, the Muslims protested against corruption and impurities that had crept into Ottoman Islam. The Muslim Arabs, no less than Balkan Christians, looked back to their medieval greatness and dreamed of independence. Peasants everywhere groped for relief from intensified feudal exploitation—this was probably the greatest source of unrest.

Hayduks, Klephts, Uskoks, Jelalis, and Levand. Violence, banditry, and general insecurity increased throughout the Empire. (*See Reading No. 11.*) This was the sign of deep malaise in the Ottoman body politic. The forces of disobedience represented nearly all social and ethnic groups. Some were "reactionary" and others "progressive"; some fought ostensibly for the preservation of the Ottoman order, and others for changing it.

Throughout the existence of the Ottoman Empire there were bands, Christians as well as Muslim, good ones and bad. Many Christians joined a rebellion when they could no longer endure Turkish oppression or when their traditional rights and privileges were taken away from them. Others went into the woods for economic reasons, to eke out a living through plunder of friend and foe alike. Some relied on indigenous support in fighting the Turks; others received aid from foreign powers. Many a *hayduk, klepht,* and *uskok* served Austria, Venice, or Russia, and the experience which they gained became useful in their later struggles for national liberation.

The Turks organized special troops to fight against criminals and rebels. Close to the Austrian and Venetian frontiers the Turks maintained military zones, broad belts of land inhabited by troops ready for instant action and enjoying special privileges in reward for their guard duties. The guards were organized to protect lines of

* The uprisings (1599-1602) led by Kara Yaziji and Deli-Hasan are particularly significant.

transportation, passes, bridges, river crossings, and the like. Whole villages were entrusted with police tasks or held collectively responsible for crimes committed.

By the eighteenth century the Ottoman Empire was honeycombed with *derebeys* (lords of the valley), who tried to carve out their own independent provinces. Some, like Ali Pasha of Ianina and Pasvanoglu of Vidin, created "independent" domains, causing much harm and embarrassment to the Sultan's authority. Janissaries and other troops often went on rampage. There were instances of merchants and soldiers attacking persons they believed to be responsible for the failing currency.

The government resorted to drastic measures to combat violence and disorder. Besides using regular and special troops in fighting unruly elements, the government issued sumptuary laws. At different times it prohibited smoking, the drinking of wine or coffee, and the wearing of "velvet garments embroidered with threads of gold" and sandals embellished with silver. Stringent regulations were posted concerning taverns, coffee houses, tobacco shops, barber shops, and bath houses. Vagabonds and "useless" people were deported, executed, or persecuted.

Arab Stirrings. Ottoman military defeats and growing contacts between the Christian subjects and Europeans, along with European incursions into the Empire, encouraged insurrectionary activity. The Capitulations of 1535 and 1740 gave the French advantages in the Empire which enabled them to extend their trade and to engage in religious proselytizing in the Levant. Jesuit, Capuchin, and Lazarist missionaries were sent there, and they founded Catholic and Uniate schools and churches.

The insurrections derived particular strength from the fact that they often combined social and economic with national and religious grievances. For a short time, a Lebanese prince, Fakhr al-Din al-Ma'ni II (1590-1635), became the lord of "Arabistan," which stretched from Aleppo to Egypt. In the middle of the eighteenth century, Wahhabism was born in the heart of Arabia. This unitarian movement called for a return to the original principles of Islam. Its founder, Muhammad ibn 'Abd al-Wahhab (d. 1792), combined with a local ruler, Muhammad ibn Sa'ud (d. 1765), who supplied the

Wahhabis with an armed force and political organization.
The Wahhabis survived Egyptian and Turkish invasions,
and their doctrines remain today as the official faith of
Saudi Arabia.

After the Turks conquered Egypt in 1517, they failed
to uproot the Mamluks, who sometimes cooperated with
the Sultan and at other times opposed him. In 1769,
under the leadership of 'Ali Bey, the Mamluks drove the
Ottoman pasha from Egypt and proclaimed their independence. 'Ali Bey established contact with the Russians,
who had entered the Mediterranean in pursuit of the
Turks, although efforts to form an effective alliance came
to naught. 'Ali Bey conquered parts of Syria and Arabia,
but his rule was shortlived; he was overthrown by a sub-
ordinate and met his death in 1773.

Napoleon's invasion of Egypt in 1798 had far-reaching consequences in the modern history of the Turks and
Arabs. The Turks, the Russians, and the English fought
side by side against Napoleon and expelled his forces
from Egypt. The leaders of the Muslim world became
divided into what Arnold Toynbee calls the zealots and
Herodians, uncompromising traditionalists and modern-
ists respectively. Muhammad 'Ali, the ruler of Egypt
(1805-1848) and founder of the dynasty that ended with
King Faruk in 1952, belonged to the latter group. He
fell under the sway of the French influence, fought the
Wahhabis for the domination of Arabia, sent his armies
into the Sudan, struggled with the Sultan over Syria
(1830-1840), and is generally considered the first Arab
potentate to espouse modernism.

The process of imperial disintegration gained momentum everywhere. Lebanon, which had enjoyed varying
degrees of self-government since the sixteenth century,
obtained further concessions after the 1840's and especially after the 1860's when it received an organic statute
granting local autonomy. Egypt's autonomy steadily expanded. Between 1831 and 1841 Muhammad 'Ali took
over control of extensive Arab territories from the Sultan
and his military victories threatened to destroy the Empire, but in the end he was forced to relinquish his ac-
quisitions by the intervention of European powers. In
1867 Egypt became a Khedivate only to fall under

British occupation in 1882 and to become a British protectorate in 1914. France acquired Algeria in 1830 and Tunisia in 1881, while Italy seized Libya in 1911.

The Eastern Question. Western ideas and Catholic missionaries came also to the Greeks and Serbs in the wake of the Austrian and Venetian invasions. From the time of Peter the Great, Russia began to show a growing interest in the Christian subjects of the Ottoman Empire and to agitate among the Balkan peoples. After the end of the eighteenth century the Turks suffered continued territorial losses. One province after another was severed from what became known as the "Sick Man" of Europe. As a result of the devastating war of 1768-1774, terminated by the Treaty of Küchük-Kaynarja, Russia extended her territory along the Black Sea, which ceased to be the Turkish lake. The Treaty recognized Russia as protector of the Orthodox believers in the Ottoman Empire and thereby gave the Tsar the right to meddle in Turkish domestic affairs. Such developments gave birth to what was called the "Eastern Question"—the struggle for the inheritance of the Turkish possessions.

The Sultan faced increasing difficulties with his rebellious subjects. The Serbs rebelled twice, under Djordje Petrović (Karadjorde) in 1804 and under Miloš Obrenović in 1815. They received partial autonomy in the Treaty of Bucharest of 1812, full autonomy in the Treaty of Adrianople of 1829, and independence from the Ottoman Empire in the Treaty of Berlin of 1878. After years of bitter fighting (1821-1828) Greece emerged as an independent state within narrow confines. She acquired Thessaly in 1881 and parts of Epirus, Macedonia, and Thrace in 1912-1913. As a result of much strife Crete won partial autonomy in 1867 and full autonomy in 1897; it became an integral part of Greece in 1912. The Rumanian principalities obtained "fuller" autonomy in 1829, *de facto* independence in 1858, and *de jure* independence in 1878. The Montenegrins engaged the Turks in many border fights, enjoying varying degrees of self-government over a long period of time, and were finally recognized as an independent state in 1878. Between 1878 and 1914 Cyprus evolved into a British crown colony. The Turks and Armenians struggled over the land each claimed as its own. Thousands of Armenians were killed in 1894-1897 and 1909, and a million and a half more in 1916. In the meantime, in 1912-1913, the Balkan states combined forces and almost evicted the Turks from Europe. As a result of its defeat in the First World War, the Ottoman Empire collapsed altogether. Out of its ruins emerged a number of successor-states and a homogeneous Turkish state based on Anatolia.

The Straits. By opening the Black Sea to trade and giving Russian merchant ships the right of passage through the Straits, the Treaty of Küchük-Kaynarja introduced the question of the Straits which in time became a major European problem. The Peace of the Dardanelles between Great Britain and Turkey (1807) established what is known as "the ancient rule" of the Ottoman Empire to close the Straits. The Treaty of Adrianople (1829) confirmed the principle that the Straits were opened only to merchant ships. A few years later the Treaty of Unkiar Skelesi (1833) opened the Straits to Russian warships but closed them to other powers. In 1835 an American frigate sought permission to pass to the Black Sea. The Porte submitted the request to the Russian ambassador, who turned it down. It was during this period that the United States became increasingly interested in Turkey. (*See Reading No. 16.*) Russia for various reasons abandoned her privileged position and signed the Treaty of London (1841) closing the Straits to foreign ships of war. The Treaty of Paris (1856) demilitarized and neutralized the Black Sea, while the London Convention (1871) abrogated this same clause and confirmed the principle established in 1841. A special clause, however, allowed the Sultan to open the Straits in time of peace to friendly warships. By a secret agreement of 1915 the Allies promised the Straits and Istanbul to Russia. The agreement was not honored because the Bolshevik Revolution (1917) put Russia out of the war, and the Bolsheviks subsequently renounced the annexation of the Straits. The Treaty of Lausanne (1924) laid down the principle of the freedom of passage, changing thereby the provisions of the Treaty of 1841. Henceforth the Straits were placed under an International Commission and demilitarized, and the non-Black Sea powers were permitted to send into the Black Sea a naval force not to exceed in size the most powerful fleet in the Black Sea.

— 9 —

REFORM AND WESTERNIZATION: ATATÜRK

Even when it became apparent that the Empire was slipping to its doom, the Ottoman rulers for a long while erected a curtain against Western ideas. Although mindful of reforms, they were less interested in borrowing from Europe than in restoring the old institutions. But the penetration of Western influence could not be stopped. Sephardic Jews from Spain and Portugal, who arrived from the late fifteenth century on, brought with them new ideas in medicine and the sciences. European civilization was also transmitted by diplomats, travelers, and merchants. The periodic occupations of Ottoman territory by Austrian, Venetian, and Russian armies left behind European ideas. Christian subjects were more receptive to these ideas than were the Muslims, but the former in turn influenced the latter.

The Beginning of Reforms. The first reforms in the Ottoman Empire were initiated by traditionalists in the time of Sultan Murad IV (1623-1640). Not until the Köprülü grand vezirs in the late seventeenth century were innovations introduced in military tactics and organization. According to Niyazi Berkes, the traditionalists erred in thinking that the restoration of the old institutions with slight changes was all that was needed "to revitalize the traditional system."

Nothing did more to convince the Turks of the superiority of many Christian institutions than the military debacles from the seventeenth century on. During the Tulip Period (so called because of the popularity of Tulip growing in the early seventeenth century) the

88

Ottomans changed their attitude toward European civilization. The era brought a close contact between the Turks and Westerners "and especially between the Turks and the French." The Grand Vezir Damad Ibrahim Pasha (1718-1730) sent a mission to Vienna and the prominent statesman Yirmisekiz Chelebi Mehmed to the court of Louis XV to study Western governments and societies. Upon returning from France Yirmisekiz Chelebi Mehmed wrote his well known *Sefaretname,* in which he described what he saw and learned. Under the vezirate of Ibrahim Pasha a modest scale of modernization was initiated. Military training on European lines was introduced in 1727. Ibrahim Müteferrika, a Hungarian Calvinist converted to Islam, founded the first Turkish printing press, but only publication of non-religious books was allowed because of the *ulema*'s insistence that printed scriptures "would no longer be scriptures." In addition to founding the press, Müteferrika drew attention to European intellectual and technological progress and cited the reformist successes of Peter the Great in Russia.

For the first time the Turkish leaders began to realize that reform should be something more than the return to the original pure Ottoman practices. Most reformers at the time were moderate. Grand Vezir Raghib Pasha (1757-1763), for example, was willing to accept technical borrowings from Europe so long as the basic Ottoman institutions were kept intact. In the meantime Western architectural styles and furnishings found their way into Istanbul. Aristocratic Turks had portraits made of themselves in the Western fashion. More and more Turks studied Western languages. The Frenchman Count de Bonneval and the Franco-Hungarian Baron de Tott were employed as instructors and technical experts. On the recommendation of the former a short-lived school of mathematics was founded in 1734, the purpose of which was to train military engineers. With the assistance of the latter, light artillery was introduced in 1774. In the time of the Grand Vezir Halil Hamid Pasha an engineering school was opened (1784). An increasing number of Ottoman citizens, especially Greeks and Armenians, traveled abroad and returned home with new ideas. Secularism and nationalism, products of the Enlightenment and the French Revolution, made headway in the Ottoman Empire. Many started to think that the future rested not with a theocratic order but with a secular society. New leaders had to be trained and a new mentality created before serious reforms could be carried out.

Selim III and His Reforms. At the end of the eighteenth century the Ottoman Empire was far behind Europe in social, economic, and political development; it was swept by social strife and political disorder. Military equipment and techniques were obsolete and the armed forces undisciplined. Many public servants were incompetent or dishonest. For the conduct of foreign affairs the Turks still relied largely on Greek and Armenian *dragomans* (translators and interpreters), who could not always be trusted. To check the dissolution of the Empire, drastic measures were needed.

The most urgent of these measures were the modernization of the armed forces and the strengthening of the central government. Selim III was convinced that reforms should not be restricted to the military, but should also recast civil and religious institutions. Moreover, he thought that such reforms should be prepared through "deliberation and universal consent," because true reforms could not be introduced by means of the traditional government apparatus. He established a consultative assembly (*mejlis-i meshveret*) under his chairmanship to discuss reform measures.

Before Selim III came to the throne he pondered reform and corresponded with Louis XVI on the subject. He propounded a program of reforms called the "New Order" (*Nizam-i Jedid*), and between 1792 and 1793 decrees were issued that brought changes in local administration and the imperial economic and military systems. Selim founded army and navy schools, brought French and English and Swedish instructors to teach the Turks modern military science, and as we have already seen, proceeded to organize a modern army. Despite powerful resistance on the part of the conservative elements, Selim pressed forward with his reforms. In 1792 the Ottoman Empire for the first time established a regular diplomatic service, and the Turkish corps of diplomats included a number of progressive men.

The activities of the *derebeys,* Napoleon's invasion of Egypt, and the Russo-Turkish war of 1806-1812 prevented the Sultan from giving his full attention to reforms. In addition, the Serbian Revolution (1804-1812) pinned down many troops. The result was that, in 1807, under strong pressure, the Sultan was obliged to disband the new army (*Nizam-i Jedid*). The opposition was not satisfied and succeeded first in deposing him and then in murdering him and dispersing his supporters. The throne was entrusted to Mustafa IV.

In the meantime, Mustafa Bayrakdar, the governor of Silistria, threw his weight behind the reform movement and with his sympathizers seized Istanbul. Mustafa IV was deposed and Mahmud II was brought to the throne. Mustafa Bayrakdar became the grand vezir. In November 1808, the Janissaries overthrew Mustafa Bayrakdar, and with his fall the first earnest attempts to reform the Empire ended abruptly.

The Tanzimat (Regulations). The second reformist movement, the *Tanzimat,* began in the final years of Mahmud II (1808-1839) and lasted until the fall of Abdul Hamid (1876-1909). It was inspired by the ruling class in the hope of saving the Empire. While ready to accept the material things of the West, the Tanzimatists questioned the applicability of Western political thought to Ottoman society. They rejected the atheism of Voltaire and Rousseau and insisted that only religion and sacred law could provide the real basis for state and society. Some, like Ahmed Atif Efendi, saw both good and bad in Western civilization; they suspected in particular the secularist and terroristic aspects of the French Revolution. Others, like Sadik Rifat Pasha (1807-1856), a diplomat in Vienna, found that material progress in the West stemmed from acceptance of the principles of liberty, equality, and the rights of the people. Sadullah Pasha (1838-1891) attributed Western successes to the "triumph of science, the rule of law, and the spread of education."

Mahmud II was a reformist by conviction. Unfortunately the powerful domestic opposition, internal strife, and the Russo-Turkish war, which was resumed in 1809, compelled him to postpone reforms. After the Treaty of Bucharest (1812) the Sultan's energy was again consumed by the Wahhabis, the Greek war of independence (1821-1829), and a new Russo-Turkish war (1828-. 1829). Yet the process of modernization continued. Shanizade (1769-1826) translated foreign works in philosophy, anatomy, medicine, and a variety of other technical subjects. Thanks to his efforts, the Ottoman Empire enjoyed the first benefits of modern medicine. The Jewish born Hoja Ishak Efendi (1774-1834), a teacher in the school of mathematics, wrote a four-volume study of mathematics and a number of other scientific treatises.

The reforms of the *Tanzimat* period affected not only state institutions, but also the everyday life of the people. Like Peter the Great of Russia, Mahmud II showed an interest in the appearance of his subjects. A decree was issued in 1829 regulating civilian dress. The North African *fez,* a red headdress of Moroccan origin, was adopted as the national headgear in place of the traditional fur-ringed *shubara*. After 1829 only the *ulema* were allowed to wear a turban and stambouline, a black frock coat. The European saddle was introduced, despite opposition in certain quarters. A dearth of capital and an unstable financial situation, however, impeded reforms. Mahmud II tried to resolve the financial situation by changing the name and value of the currency on several occasions. The piastres fell from 23 to a pound sterling in 1814 to 104 in 1839. The Ottoman Bank, founded in 1840, issued the first paper money.

The reforms introduced in education, justice, government, and the military system have been discussed elsewhere in this book. They did more to undermine the old order and its antiquated institutions and practices than to bring stability and prosperity to the country. In order to eliminate corruption from the government, a more secure tenure for its employees was provided in the time of Mahmud II. Because a strong government depended on an efficient and adequate system of communications, in 1834 a postal service was established. Since a poor transportation system obstructed commerce and hindered troop movements, the roads were improved and extended. A quarantine system was established. In 1831 the government started to publish an official gazette (*Takvim-i Vekayi*), and in 1840 the first unofficial newspaper (*Jeride-i Havadis*) appeared. Telegraphic service was introduced during the Crimean War, and the first railway (*Izmir-Aydin*) was built in 1866.

Hatt-i Sherif of Gülhane and Hatt-i Humayun. After Mahmud's reforms the question was no longer whether or not to reform the Empire, but how to do it. In 1839 the Sultan Abdul Mejid issued the Noble Decree of the Rose Chamber (*Hatt-i Sherif of Gülhane*)—the Ottoman "Bill of Rights." (*See Reading No. 13.*) The document was largely the work of Mustafa Reshid Pasha (1800-1858), son of a *vakf* official, who was the Turkish ambassador in France and later foreign minister. The reform decree promised "perfect security for life, honor, and fortune" to all Ottoman subjects. Tax-farming was abolished, and a system for regular and orderly recruitment of men for the armed forces was introduced. The equality of all Ottoman subjects was proclaimed. The most significant result of the *Hatt* of 1839 was not the half-hearted implementation of reforms, but the psychological impact on the subject peoples, who became even more determined to achieve their aspirations.

During the Crimean War (1853-1856) there was strong pressure on the Porte to adopt reforms that would guarantee equality to all citizens. This course of action was urged by enlightened Turks such as Ali Pasha* and Fuad Pasha,† by the spokesmen of the oppressed peoples, and by the representatives of the allied powers. Finally, in exchange for admission into the concert of Europe, the Turks agreed to issue "as a spontaneous act of the sultan" a new reform charter, the Imperial Decree (*Hatt-i Humâyun*) of February 18, 1856. (*See Reading No. 13.*) The charter was ceremoniously proclaimed by the Sultan before the grand vezir and many notables, includ-

---

* Ali Pasha served as the first chairman of the High Council of Reform and subsequently as grand vezir.
† Fuad Pasha, a graduate of the medical school, after diplomatic service abroad became foreign minister under Ali Pasha in 1852.

ing the Greek and Armenian patriarchs and the Jewish
grand rabbi. A special treaty, concluded between Turkey
and the powers on March 30, admitted the former to the
Concert of Europe and bound the latter to defend Ottoman independence and integrity.

One difference between the 1839 and 1856 decrees
was that the first originated at home and the second
abroad. Otherwise they had a great deal in common. The
Hatt of 1856 confirmed the promises of the 1839 document—the abolition of tax-farming and bribery, and
military and judicial equality. It contained provisions
that were absent in the earlier one: strict adherence to
the annual budget, establishment of banks, employment
of European capital, codification of penal and commercial law, prison reform, establishment of mixed courts,
prohibition of the use of insulting epithets, and abandonment of the death sentence for apostacy to Islam. The
Hatt of 1856 further promised improved provincial and
communal councils which would extend the principle of
representation. It provided for the reorganization of the
millet system in such a way as to give the secular element
a greater say in *millet* affairs. The Supreme Council of
Judicial Ordinances was broadened to include non-Muslim representatives. The *Hatt* of 1856 initiated a second
phase of Europeanization. According to Davison all
major reforms introduced from now until the issuance of
the Constitution of 1876 "were aimed at preserving the
empire."

On different occasions the Powers complained to the
Porte about the failure to implement the promised reforms. Yet considering the internal difficulties in the
1860's—violence in Lebanon, border warfare with Montenegro, crises in Serbia, Egypt, Crete, and Armenia—
it is remarkable how much was done. The Porte was
particularly plagued with financial problems. The currency continued to drop in value, and in 1858 the Porte
was forced to contract a foreign loan in order to stabilize
finances. This temporary transfusion failed to dispel the
financial troubles, and new foreign loans had to be obtained. Nevertheless, the reforms were continued.

The Vilayet Law of 1864. The Vilayet Law of 1864
was more important than the *millet* constitutions because

it affected the lives of all imperial subjects regardless of their confession.* Grand Vezir Fuad and Midhat Pasha, then a territorial governor, were principally responsible for the Vilayet Law, which had been promised in the reform decree of 1856. Before its enactment it was tested successfully in two of the most difficult territories, Tuna and Baghdad vilayets. The Law, which was revised in 1867 and 1871, regrouped the existing territories (*eyalets*) into 27 larger territorial units (*vilayets*), each headed by a governor (*vali*) who recruited his own staff and possessed extensive powers. The territorial government was made up of departments in charge of civil, financial, police, judicial, and certain other affairs. The head of the department of finance was directly responsible to the minister of finance in Istanbul.

Under the new law the territories were subdivided into departments (*sanjaks*), which differed from the old feudal types. The departments were subdivided into districts (*kazas*), and the districts, into communes (*nahiye*) and villages. The head of a department was a *mutasarrif;* of a district, a *kaymakam;* of a commune, a *mudir;* and of a village or settlement, a *mukhtar.*

The Vilayet Law provided for the establishment of administrative councils (*mejlis-i dare*) with deliberative and advisory functions at provincial, departmental, and district levels. The council members were chosen by councils of elders (*ihtiyar mejlisi*) made up of religious heads and elected members. The local officials sat in the administrative councils as ex-officio members. Though the system was much improved over the one introduced by Reshid Pasha, it left much to be desired. Through an ingenious electoral system the Porte was able to control the elections. The arrangement assured the Muslims of a council majority even in regions in which Christians were the dominant population. Moreover, the Istanbul-appointed officials had the decisive voice in local government.

The Vilayet Law also provided for the establishment of the general assembly (*mejlis-i umumi*) in each prov-

---

* Compare with the earlier discussion of regional government and *millets.*

ince, consisting of four elected representatives from each department (two Muslims and two non-Muslims). The Law provided for a mixed civil and criminal court in each province, department, and district. The court consisted of three Muslims and three non-Muslims, and was presided over by a nominee of Sheykh ul-Islam. The court and the general assembly were more nearly representative than the administrative councils, although their members were selected under the close watch of the Porte's officials.

Some aspects of the new administrative organization resembled the French system. France was the source of inspiration for the Turkish reformers, and Sultan Abdul Aziz himself was in many ways an admirer of France. In 1867, on the invitation of the French government, the Sultan visited Paris, London, and Vienna, the first of the Ottoman rulers to undertake such a journey.

The New Ottomans (Yeni Osmanlilar). The most vigorous exponents of the reforms from the 1860's until the 1880's was a group of intellectuals called the New Ottomans. At a picnic in the summer of 1866, in the Forest of Belgrade not far from Istanbul, six young men decided to launch a concerted drive for reform. The leader of the group was Mehmed Bey, who had been educated at the Ottoman school in Paris. The group decided to organize a secret society called the Patriotic Alliance (*Ittifak-i Hamiyet*) modeled on the Young Italy movement, and its members became known as the New Ottomans.

The New Ottomans disagreed with the *Tanzimat* objective of reforming the Empire while preserving the old social system and with the idea that the ruling classes should be responsible for the institution of reforms. The New Ottomans wanted to secure political and social equality for all Ottoman subjects, to restrict the powers of autocracy by a fundamental law, and to cope with the restless minorities by a policy of "Ottomanization." Mardin traces every area of modernization in contemporary Turkey to the New Ottomans, who were the first of the Turkish intelligentsia to make use of "the media of mass communication to voice extremely articulate criticisms of the government."

The philosophy of the New Ottomans was principally that of three men: Ibrahim Shinasi (1826-1871), Ziya Pasha (1825-1880), and Namik Kemal (1840-1888). They founded the "new literature" and supplied the political thought that was adopted by future generations of Turkish thinkers. Shinasi was a poet, dramatist, and journalist who translated French literary works and wrote "The Marriage of a Poet," the first original Turkish play. Shinasi was in a position to encourage reforms because he held various government posts and was a friend of Reshid Pasha, the reformist grand vezir. After losing his government job Shinasi gave himself largely to literature, publishing the journal called *Tasvir-i Efkar,* the first Turkish paper to publish an intelligent analysis of domestic and foreign affairs. In 1867 Shinasi fled to Paris.

In 1854, through the influence of Reshid Pasha, Ziya Pasha was appointed a secretary to the Sultan. He mastered French and translated French works into Turkish. Like others who shared his thoughts, he was forced to flee to Western Europe in 1867. During his stay abroad Ziya lived in Paris, London, and Geneva. After the death of the Grand Vezir Ali Pasha, who distrusted him, Ziya returned to Turkey and was named governor of Syria.

The most outspoken exponent of patriotism and liberalism during this period was Namik Kemal, an admirer of Montesquieu and Rousseau. He published numerous newspaper articles and in 1863 started to translate Montesquieu's *Spirit of Laws* with the aim of showing that the ideas of the Frenchman were not incompatible with the Muslim Sacred Law. In a visionary dialogue entitled "Dream," Namik Kemal expressed a wish for a constituent assembly, but this was the most radical step he was ready to take. Of what he saw in Europe, the English form of government and civilization impressed him the most. Namik Kemal was the prime force of the New Ottomans, and after Mehmed Bey was the most important of them. After Shinasi fled abroad Namik Kemal was entrusted with the publication of the *Tasvir-i Efkar.*

Among other prominent New Ottomans was Ali Suavi, who was the editor of *The Informer (Muhbir),* which appeared for the first time in early 1867. Ali Suavi's articles were critical of the government, for which reason he was banished to Anatolia, whence he escaped to Europe.

While in Paris, the New Ottomans made their headquarters in the residence of Prince Mustafa Fazil, brother of the Khedive Ismail of Egypt and son of Ibrahim Pasha. They organized a new society in May, 1867, and chose Ziya Bey as its head. Ali Sauvi revived *Muhbir*, which became the society's organ, but close French surveillance compelled them to issue the paper in London instead of Paris. The first issue, therefore, did not appear until August 31, 1867. The refugees, some more radical in their thinking than others, were unable to agree among themselves. Squabbles led Kemal and his supporters to publish their own paper, the well known *Freedom (Hürriyet)*, which appeared for the first time in June, 1868.

Prince Fazil was the most unsteady of the New Ottomans, always ready to forego principles for personal advantage. When he decided to abandon the cause and return to Turkey, the New Ottomans shifted their base of operations to London. Most of them, including Namik Kemal, returned home after the death of the Grand Vezir Ali Pasha in 1871.

Upon his return to Turkey, Namik Kemal started a paper called *Ibret* with the support of Ebüzziya Tevfik (1849-1913), the author of the history of the New Ottoman movement. The printing plant was supplied by Prince Mustafa Fazil. The paper gave much of its space to the problem of Islamic union. Namik Kemal's patriotic drama, *Vatan* (which appeared in 1873), and activities of the New Ottomans caused so much excitement that the authorities decided to take repressive measures. *Ibret* was suspended in April, 1873, and the New Ottomans banished. Namik Kemal was sent to Cyprus, Ebüzziya and Ahmed Midhat to Rhodes, and others to Acre. Not until Sultan Abdul Aziz fell from power in 1876 were they amnestied and allowed to return home.

The New Ottomans were the first to attempt a synthesis of the ideas of the European Enlightenment and Islam. Berkes contends that like the *Tanzimat* reformers, they failed because they wanted neither to modernize the Ottoman state nor to revitalize Islam, being satisfied merely with stripping religion of its political support. The result was a form of modern society neither genuinely Islamic nor genuinely Western. Since the *Tanzimat* reformers considered the modern state and Islam incompatible, they endeavored to keep them apart.

The work of the New Ottomans is not to be underestimated for it was important in galvanizing the opponents of Abdul Hamid to action, and there is a definite link between them and the Young Turks and Atatürk who followed.

Nationalism. Fostered by the ideas of the French Revolution and German romanticism, nationalism was slow in coming to the Turks. By the end of the eighteenth century, however, nationalism had reached several of the Turkish subject peoples. For the first time in the nineteenth century the Turks began to think of themselves not only as Muslims, but also as Turks in the modern concept of nationalism. Disgraced by Russian victories on land and sea in the war of 1768-1774, the Turks were forced to hand over to Russia the Turkic-Tartar Muslims of Crimea. This and the fact that the Sultan was obliged to recognize Russia as protector of his Orthodox subjects was very much resented by the Turks. While the subject peoples equated nationalism with independence and sought freedom from feudal and religious oppression, the Turks looked at nationalism as a means by which they could defeat despotism and assure themselves of continued hegemony within the Empire. The two kinds of nationalism were irreconcilable.

Turkish nationalism was manifested in different forms. The *Tanzimat* reformers, including the New Ottomans, supported the cause of Ottomanism, the doctrine that all subjects of the Empire, regardless of their ethnic or confessional background, were Ottomans, members of the same community. But Ottomanism was understood differently by different thinkers. The conception of it held by the *Tanzimat* statesmen was "Turkish-colored." Ottomanism did not take root because it was rejected by many subject nations and because its principal supporters disagreed over its implementation. Ahmed Midhat

(1844-1912), a journalist, novelist, and historian, abandoned the cause and decided to collaborate with the authorities. Ebüzziya Tevfik, the publisher and historian, took the same course. There were other similar examples of ideological meanderings on the part of the Turkish liberals.

Pan-Islamism and Pan-Turkism. After the 1870's Turkish liberals gave much thought to two new concepts. The first of these was Pan-Islamism (*see Reading No. 15*), which evolved over the years and was given a theoretical basis by Jamal al-Din al-Afghani (1838-1896). At the end of the eighteenth century some Turkish thinkers began to see an opportunity for the Sultan, in his capacity as the Caliph, to save his Empire by championing world-wide Muslim solidarity against Western encroachment. Concern over the Empire's future led Selim III (1789-1808) and his successors to assert themselves as caliphs. Probably in the time of Selim III developed the legend that the descendant of the Abbasids at the Mamluk court in Egypt surrendered the caliphal prerogatives to Selim I. There is no evidence that any Sultan before Selim III claimed the title of Caliph, and in fact no Sultan until Abdul Hamid II (1876-1909) used it for political purposes.

Jamal al-Din al-Afghani, a Pan-Islamist and a liberal modernist, advocated modernization of Muslim states by adoption of Western scientific achievements, a common struggle against English, French, and Russian imperialism, and Muslim union under one caliphate. Abdul Hamid II endeavored by various means to secure the support of Jamal al-Din for his own brand of Pan-Islam, which would confirm him as the Caliph of all the Muslims and serve Ottoman political interests. Many Ottomans saw in Pan-Islamism an effective way to weaken Russia. Others saw it as an answer to growing Arab nationalism. The Indian and Russian Muslim leaders pinned the hopes of their peoples to Pan-Islamism and deliberately fanned it.

Another concept, Pan-Turkism (*see Reading No. 15*), especially espoused by the Turks in Russia (e.g., the Tatar Akjuraoglu Yusuf), called for the unity of all Turks. The Ottoman Turks began to show greater interest in the fate of their co-nationals in Russia in the 1870's when the Tsarist government pressed the conquest of Central Asia. Some of the New Ottomans, like Ali Suavi, wrote on the subject and tried to interest the government in Russian Turks. Like Pan-Islamism, Pan-Turkism had many sympathizers but never developed into an effective political movement. There are still persons in Turkey and in the Soviet Union who hope to unite all the Turks. Pan-Turkism elicited suspicion among the non-Turkish elements of the Empire and further alienated them from Ottoman rule. Neither Pan-Islamism nor Pan-Turkism seemed to be the solution for the Ottoman multinational state.

Economic Crisis. Since the Crimean War the Porte had taken out 10 loans under onerous conditions, paying an average interest of 9½ per cent. The outstanding debt, increased by recent purchases of armored ships and guns (from Krupp), was estimated at more than 6¼ billion francs. Attempts to negotiate a new loan in Paris and to make the Ottoman Bank the tax-collector-general of the Empire were not successful. As the expenses of the state and of the court steadily mounted, the Sultan declared bankruptcy in October, 1875. The Russian ambassador, who saw an opportunity to harm Western creditors, encouraged the Sultan to suspend the payment of interest on the imperial debt. The Porte announced that for the next five years it would be able to pay on loans (excepting the first two loans and certain state papers) only half of the interest in cash and the other half in 5 per cent bonds.

Constitution. By the 1870's a few Turkish leaders were convinced that more than a mere "patching up" of the decrepit theocratic regime was needed. The more the Porte conceded to its discontented subjects, the more their appetites were whetted. It began to appear that only herculean measures could resolve the imperial crisis.

Some Ottomans thought that the establishment of a constitutional government could avert the imminent collapse of the Empire. One of the most influential constitutionalists was Midhat Pasha, who had demonstrated the value of reforms as governor of the Danubian vilayet. A staunch exponent of Ottomanism, Midhat Pasha envisaged a parliament that would include representatives of all the diverse nationalities in the Empire.

On October 9, 1876, a constitutional committee was appointed to draft a constitutiôn. The New Ottomans had an active part in this work, Ziya being made the chairman of the subcommittee and Namik Kemal a member of it. By the end of November the draft was submitted to the Sultan, and on December 23, at the very time when European representatives had assembled at Constantinople to decide the fate of the Empire, the first Ottoman constitution was promulgated. The Sultan appointed Midhat Pasha to the office of Grand Vezir.

While the timing of the announcement may have been chosen to embarrass the European representatives at the conference and to paralyze their action, the issuance of the constitution was apparently carefully thought out by the Sultan. In a recent study Robert Devereux supplies an able discussion of the constitutional struggle in Turkey and the constitution itself. The Constitution of 1876 provided the fullest safeguards for the Sultan and his family. It declared that Ottoman sovereignty and "the Supreme Caliphate of Islam" were vested in the sultan (of the house of Osman), who was described as the "protector of the Muslim religion" and the "Sovereign and Padishah of all the Ottomans." The sultan was assured a personal protection from abuse, and property belonging to the dynasty was guaranteed. The sultan could appoint and dismiss ministers, he was in command of the armed forces, and he was in general charged with the usual functions of a chief of state.

The constitution proclaimed all Ottomans equal and declared personal liberty inviolable. While protecting the free exercise of all faiths, it established Islam as the state religion. The Constitution promised a free prcss and free education. All citizens were declared competent to hold public office, provided they knew Turkish, which was made the official language. Equitable taxation was prescribed. The right to own property and the inviolability of domiciles were guaranteed.

The Constitution of 1876 called for a modern judicial system and for provincial, departmental, and distinct councils. There was to be a bicameral leigslature. The members of the upper house, or senate, were appointed by the sultan for life. One deputy, serving for four years, was elected to the lower house for each 50,000 inhabitants.

The proclamation of the constitution, the highest achievement of the New Ottomans, threw the European conference in Constantinople into confusion. The demands that the Porte grant extensive concessions to its rebellious subjects were rejected, and the war which had broken out in the summer of 1876 between Turkey and the Balkan states of Serbia and Montenegro was resumed. Efforts by the powers to prevent the spread of the war failed, and in April, 1877, Russia and Turkey were once again involved in a military struggle.

In the meantime, amidst great expectations, haphazard elections were held and the parliament convened in March, 1877. The deputies, although inexperienced and uninformed, at once betrayed independence. The Sultan was quick to recognize dangers inherent in the parliament as deputies from different regions complained about conditions in the country; he put the Constitution aside and dissolved the parliament on February 14, 1878. Abdul Hamid dismissed and banished Midhat Pasha, who was eventually strangled in the dungeons of Arabia. Ten months of constitutional government ended abruptly, and with this the period of Tanzimat came to a close.

The *Tanzimat* reforms failed to develop a sense of Ottomanism among Turks and the subject people. What they did was to create institutional dualism—the old Turkish and new European institutions existing side by side. Important changes, however, were effected in the notion of the state and ruler. The Sultan no longer governed through officials holding almost unlimited powers (grand vezir, sheykh ul-Islam), but through ministers with greatly circumscribed powers. The indirect *Muquata's* system of administration was replaced by a direct one consisting of paid officials responsible to the central government. Finally, the *Tanzimat* period brought secular statesmen and intelligentsia into the government.

Hamidian Despotism. Restoration of the Constitution became the battle cry of the political opposition. This convinced the Sultan that he must destroy his political enemies. Many of the erstwhile New Ottomans were placed under police surveillance. The political situation grew tense. In August, 1878, Ali Suavi led an unsuccessful attack on the palace; he was captured and executed. Ziya Pasha fell into disfavor in 1881 and died a disillusioned man while serving as governor of Adana. Namik Kemal was banished and died on the Island of Chios in 1888. Aziz Bey, a high official of the Inspectorate of Evkaf, a Greek called Cleanthe Scalieri, and some Freemasons organized a committee whose purpose was to overthrow the Sultan.

The Sultan was surrounded by sycophants and lived in mortal fear of his subjects. His despotic rule, operating through espionage and police, disillusioned even his friends. State officials began to conspire against the Sultan. The teachers in their classrooms discussed the forbidden works of Namik Kemal, Ziya Pasha, and other political thinkers and writers. By the beginning of the 1890's the rigors of government control and financial difficulties forced all but two of the six major papers, *Perservering* (*Ikdam*) and *Morning* (*Sabah*), to go out of business.

The wars with Russia, Montenegro, and Serbia depleted the meager finances of the Empire, and on December 20, 1881, Sultan Abdul Hamid issued a decree putting into effect an arrangement made with bondholders' groups whereby the country's foreign debt was reduced to 106 million pounds. Certain revenues (from salt, tobacco, stamps, fees on alcohol, silk, etc.) were henceforth to be used in payment of the debt. The Council of Administration of the Ottoman Public Debt was authorized to collect revenues and taxes on behalf of the bondholders. The Council consisted of seven members, only one of them appointed by the Sultan, the rest b ing appointees of the Ottoman Bank, which was controlled by the British and the French. Many of the best jobs in the Administration were held by foreigners.

The Ottoman Public Debt Administration was more than a banking and collecting agency. Under it Ottoman Finances were stabilized, improvements in production of silk made, and the construction of railways facilitated. Functioning as an instrument of foreign economic and political intrusion, the Administration was resented by many Turks. Nonetheless, it survived until the end of the First World War.

Despite his rule, Abdul Hamid did not advocate return to the old ways. He honored most of the reforms already introduced and himself encouraged the modernization of the Empire. In this he had the strong support of the Grand Vezir Mehmed Said Pasha (1838-1914). Many schools were built, and communications and transportation facilities were extended.

The Young Turk Movement. In May, 1889, a group of students at the Imperial Military Medical School formed a revolutionary society with the purpose of overthrowing the Sultan. They came from different ethnic backgrounds. The official name of the revolutionary society was the Committee of Union and Progress (*Ittihad ve Terekki*). The members called themselves the Young Turks. In his excellent study of the Young Turks E. E. Ramsaur shows how the movement grew out of the seeds planted by the New Ottomans. Like the New Ottomans, the Young Turks were organized along the cellular lines of the Italian *Carbonari*. The principal figure in the Young Turk movement was an Albanian named Ibrahim Temo, or Edhem, as he was sometimes known. The movement enlisted supporters within the Military Medical School, which "has the historical honor of starting almost every new movement," and other centers of learning.

Sultan Abdul Hamid learned of the society's existence in 1892, and as the police began to track down its members more and more of them went abroad, concentrating for the most part in Paris. There the newcomers met Ahmed Riza (1859-1930), a member of the abortive parliament of 1877 who left Turkey in 1889. Attracted by the philosophy of Auguste Comte, Ahmed Riza circulated in Positivist circles. Together with Halil Ganem, a Christian Syrian from Beirut, who had published *Hilâl* (*The Crescent*) in Geneva, and later *La Turquie* in Paris, he started the paper *Meshveret* (*Consultation*). Besides Comte, Emile Durkheim and Henri Bergson seem also to have influenced the political thinking of the Young Turks.

As the official organ of the Committee of Union and Progress, *Meshveret* in its first issue carried the program of the organization, which called for the equality of all Ottoman subjects and peaceful and orderly reforms. The Committee opposed foreign intervention in the internal affairs of the Ottoman Empire, and what it wanted was the Ottomanization of the Empire. Copies of the *Meshveret* found their way into Turkey. Sometime in the mid-1890's Murad Bey, a teacher, arrived in Egypt and started to publish still another anti-Hamidian journal, *Mizan* (*The Scales*), which soon became more popular than the *Meshveret*. In 1895 the government began to arrest persons suspected of subversive activities.

An abortive attempt in August, 1896, by the Young Turks of Istanbul to seize the government led to a split in the ranks of its followers over tactics and ideology. Many Young Turks fell into police hands, and several of those who were abroad decided to abandon the struggle against the Sultan. Murad was one of them. These developments were a serious setback for the Young Turks' cause. The split between Murad and Ahmed Riza was an especially heavy blow to the Young Turks, but they gradually recovered.

In Geneva, in May, 1897, two Young Turks started a new organ of the society (*Osmanli,* or *Ottoman*), which appeared until 1899. Of no small psychological import was the flight to Paris, in 1899, of Damad Mahmud Pasha, the Sultan's brother-in-law, with his two sons, the Princes Sabah al-Din and Lutfallah. Damad Mahmud established contacts with Ahmed Riza and offered his cooperation. In the meantime the refugees swelled the number of the Young Turks. One of the newcomers was Ismail Kemal Bey, an Albanian who at different times held important positions in the government.

In time Prince Sabah al-Din turned into a strong rival of Ahmed Riza. The attempt at the first Congress of the Ottoman Liberals, held in Paris in February, 1902, to bring the Young Turk factions together was unsuccessful. The delegates at the Congress, including representatives of different ethnic groups, disagreed on the question of Ottoman federation and foreign guarantees of reforms in the Ottoman Empire. Prince Sabah al-Din, who had been elected president of the Congress, considered European guarantees indispensable, while Ahmed Riza felt that European intervention would be in violation of Ottoman sovereignty.

Unable to reach an agreement with Ahmed Riza, the Prince founded an organization called the League for Private Initiative and Decentralization and began to publish his own journal (*Terekki,* or *Progress*). He considered it his principal task to promote cooperation between the diverse races of the Empire. The Prince's federation plan failed to win the support of the Christian nationalities, which by this time looked for the fulfillment of their aspirations in national states.

The secret society which in 1908 "precipitated the revolution" was not an affiliate of the organizations of the exiled Young Turks. Nor was it, according to Ramsaur, "a direct heritage of any earlier Young Turk organization within the Ottoman Empire." After the debacle of 1896 revolutionary organization of any importance was possible only outside Constantinople. In October, 1906, Mustafa Kemal, later known as Atatürk, helped form a secret society known as "The Fatherland" (*Vatan*) in Damascus, where he was on military duty. The society soon had branches in Jaffa and Jerusalem, and because of special conditions in Macedonia—the war between different national bands, the province's proximity to Europe, and Salonika's reputation as "the most advanced" city in the Ottoman Empire—it was decided to extend the society's work to that province. Mustafa Kemal took sick leave to visit Salonika, his birthplace, and while there he founded a branch of "The Fatherland" society—"The Fatherland and Liberty" (*Vatan ve Hürriyet*).

After his transfer to Salonika in 1907, Mustafa Kemal discovered that another society, the Ottoman Society of Liberty (*Osmanli Hürriyet Jemiyet*), had been organized in the Third Army Corps, and he joined it. This organization and the one he founded were merged to form the "Committee of Union and Progress" which at once began to establish branches. Its influence spread rapidly.

While the Young Turk movement was coming back

to life in the Ottoman Empire, Ahmed Riza and Sabah al-Din continued to gain followers from among the latest refugees. The Turkish refugees were more attracted to "the frankly Turkish nationalism of Ahmed Riza's Committee of Union and Progress than to the idealism of Sabah al-Din's League of Administrative Decentralization and Private Initiative." The gap between Ahmed Riza and Sabah al-Din became unbridgeable.

At the second Congress of Ottoman Liberals, held in Paris in December, 1907, it was agreed to change the Ottoman government by violence if necessary. Ahmed Riza, who previously had rejected the use of violence in achieving political objectives, compromised on this occasion. A Permanent Committee was chosen to implement the program adopted at the Congress.

The Revolution of 1908.   After the bloody 1903 uprising in Macedonia the European powers agreed on a program of reforms in that province which they hoped would eliminate the source of popular discontent. Nominally under the leadership of Hilmi Pasha, the reform program got nowhere. When the King of England and the Russian Tsar met at Reval in the summer of 1908 to discuss further reforms for the Ottoman Empire, the Young Turks officers interpreted this as a threat of renewed intervention in Ottoman affairs and mutinied. A number of officers, including Enver Bey and Ahmed Niyazi, deserted their posts and took to the woods where they organized groups of irregulars. The Sultan sent Shemsi Pasha to establish order, but the insurgents assassinated him. Many of the troops employed against the insurgents defected to them. The insurgents, in control of Macedonia, threatened to march on Istanbul. As the mutiny spread, the Committee of Union and Progress came out into the open and demanded the restoration of the Constitution of 1876. With no choice left, on July 23 the Sultan granted the constitution, which was a modified version of the 1876 document. With this the Hamidian despotism ended, and a parliamentary government on the European model was instituted. The Young Turks, the term soon to become idiomatic in English, at last saw their dreams realized. Ahmed Riza became the president of the parliament.

The revolution generated a great deal of optimism. The Christian bands in Macedonia laid down their arms. Arabs began to advocate a transformation of the Empire into a dual Arab-Turkish state. Many Armenians, Kurds, and others naively expected a recognition of their national rights. Indeed the impact of the revolution of 1908 on the Ottoman peoples was profound, but not everyone approved of it or attached the same significance to it. Some Turks saw the revolution as a treacherous work of the subject peoples, although the revolution was primarily the work of Turkish officers and men. Those who sympathized with the revolution exaggerated its accomplishments.

The Counter Revolution. The Committee of Union and Progress was too weak to take firm hold of the government and to grapple successfully with the numerous state problems. The bulk of the masses still revered the Sultan-Caliph, who, in April, 1909, attempted with his supporters to overthrow the Young Turk government. Enver Pasha countered by leading the units of the Third Army Corps on Istanbul and seizing the government. The Sultan was deposed and his brother Mehmed V brought to the throne. The old Sultan was imprisoned in Salonika and removed from there in 1912 when the city fell to the Greeks. Except for a brief period, the Young Turks held control of the government until 1918. From the very start, however, two tendencies were manifest in the Young Turk movement: a liberal group which advocated the equality of all subjects of the Empire under a centralized government, and a group which stood for Turkish hegemony in the Ottoman Empire. Out of the former group emerged the Liberal Party of 1908 (*Ahrar*) and the Liberal Union of 1911.

Once in full command of the government, the Young Turks revealed their true colors. They prohibited associations based on ethnic or national affiliations and closed minority clubs and societies. The government organized special combat units to fight guerrillas and introduced heavy penalties against those caught possessing arms. It resorted to gerrymandering and pressure methods to insure Turkish control of both houses of parliament. The

Young Turks abandoned Ottomanism in favor of a policy of Turkification.

The changes in Young Turk policy shocked many who had supported them, and the feelings of hope and confidence gave way to bitterness. Italy took advantage of Ottoman instability to seize Libya* in 1911. In May, 1912, a group called the Savior Officers seized power and formed a government of their own under Gazi Ahmed Muhtar Pasha.

The Triumvirate. The defeats suffered by the Turkish armies in the First Balkan War (1912-1913) discredited the government, and in January, 1913, the Committee of Union and Progress, led by Enver Pasha, regained power. From then on the fate of Turkey rested in the hands of a triumvirate consisting of Enver Pasha, Talat Pasha, and Jemal Pasha. Enver became War Minister in 1913, Talat served as Minister of the Interior, and after 1916 as grand vezir, and Jemal was military governor of Istanbul and Minister of the Navy. The Young Turks were either unable or unwilling to introduce basic reforms. The Muslim Sacred Law remained in force, and so did the *millet* system. Religious and secular laws, caliphate and constitution, tradition and modernism were recognized. This duality proved unworkable. Despite the existence of strong nationalist movements among the subject peoples the Young Turks were determined not to weaken the Empire nor the Turkish hold over it. But the Young Turks were ideologically divided. Some were exponents of Ottomanism, others of Pan-Islamism, and still others, like Enver Bey, advocates of Pan-Turkism. The Young Turks' apologists say that they needed years of peace to build and this they did not get.

Although they denied Turkey a democratic government, the Young Turks did introduce many important measures. Particularly noteworthy were the attempts to improve the provincial administration, the police, and the transportation and communications systems. The Young Turks adopted a policy of economic nationalism, considered the possibility of reforming the system of land tenure, and encouraged the modernization of nearly every aspect of daily life. During their ascendancy one

* Tripolitania and Cyrenaica.

witnessed an outburst of unprecedented intellectual activity as voices long silenced found an audience. Literature began to prosper, and the positivist ideas of August Comte took root. The first theoretical formulation of Turkish nationalism appeared at this time. Secularism received impetus as Islamic traditionalism gave ground. Newspaper circulation increased markedly.

The First World War brought about an important social revolution in the lives of the Turks. The status of women was improved. The women took positions in the national economy previously occupied by men only, and in styles and modes they began to imitate their Christian counterparts.

The First World War. In the beginning, Turkey seemed reluctant to enter the World War which broke out in 1914. A segment of the officer corps prominent in the Committee of Union and Progress, however, had fallen under the German spell. The War Minister, Enver Pasha, was pro-German. In 1914, German agents and the German ambassador, Baron von Wagenheim, left no stone unturned to bring Turkey into the war on the side of Germany. (*See Reading No. 18.*)

Attempts by Western diplomats to prevent the Turks from joining the Central Powers failed. On August 2 Turkey and Germany signed a secret military convention. The British admiral A. H. Limpus, who had been entrusted with the organization of the Turkish navy, was replaced by a German admiral, Souchon, who took over the direction of the Turkish marine forces just as the German general Liman von Sanders had taken command of the army. By October German officers had ciosed the Straits and ordered a bombardment of Russian ports by warships which had been turned over to the Turks. The Russians declared war on Turkey on November 4, and England and France immediately followed suit.

England and Russia sought to enlist the support of discontented Ottoman subjects. England concentrated on the Arabs, and the Russians on the Armenians. On November 14, the Sultan proclaimed the "Holy War" (*Jihad*), confident in the power of Pan-Islamism. He hoped that the Muslim faithful would respond to the call, especially the Muslims of Russia, British India, and French

North Africa, and his own Arab subjects. The response was feeble. The Sharif Husein, in charge of the holy city of Mecca, turned a deaf ear, and ultimately chose the British as his allies.

Early in the war the Turks, backed by the Germans, fought on three fronts—Suez, Mesopotamia, and Eastern Anatolia—and were initially successful. The British and French landed on the peninsula of Gallipoli at the entrance to the Dardanelles in January, 1915, in an attempt to separate Turkey from Germany, to establish contact with Russia, and to keep that country in the war, but Turkish and German artillery compelled them to withdraw in January, 1916. The Allies then established a foothold on Greek soil at Salonika.

Collapse. Had it not been for the Russian Revolutions of February and October, 1917, Turkish defenses might have weakened sooner than they did. As it was, Russia was forced to withdraw from eastern Anatolia, and the Turks surged forward to occupy several districts. The Treaty of Brest-Litovsk (March 3, 1918), which took Russia formally out of the war, left the Turks in possession of Kars, Ardahan, and Batum.

However, the resumption of the British offensives in Mesopotamia and Palestine, coupled with the Arab Revolt against the Sultan which began in the summer of 1916, was too much for the Turks. Despite German reinforcements the Turks began to yield ground, and finally the Ottoman government collapsed. The new government of the Liberal Union was made up of persons ready to sue for peace. Sultan Vahideddin, or Mehmed VI, remained at the helm. On October 30, 1918, at Mudros, the Turks signed the armistice ending the war. the "Sick Man of Europe" finally expired. The Triumvirate that had led the country into war took to its heels. Enver Pasha found his way to Russia, where he led the Bashmachis of Central Asia against the Bolsheviks and was killed in 1922 in Turkestan. An Armenian assassin cut down Talat Pasha in Berlin, and Jemal Pasha entered the Afghan military service.

Mustafa Kemal Atatürk. In a memorandum written in 1822, Akif Efendi observed that the Ottomans could either champion Islam, submit to foreign rule, or retreat into the Anatolian "heartland." The first two, as well as Pan-Turkism, proved unworkable, leaving the third the only realistic choice. In 1918 the Turks found their destiny in a nationally homogeneous Turkish state, based on Turkism (*Türkiye Jelik*)—an ethnic and cultural unity of the Ottoman Turks. A new philosophy was formulated by Ziya Gökalp. (*See Reading No. 14.*) He said: "A Nation is not a racial, ethnic, geographical, political or voluntary group or association. A Nation is a group composed of men and women who have gone through the same education, who have received the same acquisition in language, religion, morality and aesthetics."

Turkism represented a blend of liberal Ottoman nationalism (of Shinasi, Ziya, and Kemal) and Turkish nationalism (of Vefik, Suavi, and Gökalp). It was personified by Mustafa Kemal (later to be called Atatürk), the founder of modern Turkey, who modified Gökalp's nationalism by secularizing the government and limiting Turkey's territorial claims. (*See Reading No. 19.*) He saw the only hope for the Turks in withdrawal to Anatolia, where the Turks lived in a compact mass and possessed a common culture.

Who was this Mustafa Kemal Atatürk? He was born in Salonika in 1888. His father was a minor official. Mustafa was a good student; he learned French, and studied at the military academy. Later he was active as a Young Turk conspirator. Until the World War he was not well known, being overshadowed by such prominent military men as Enver Bey. The war brought him into the limelight because of his bravery at Gallipoli in 1915 and on the Caucasian front. Enver Bey honored him by giving him command of the army and the title of pasha. But as the war progressed he became disillusioned with Enver, Talat, and Jemal, who allowed the Germans to convert Turkey into an instrument of their military and economic objectives. Mustafa Kemal had resigned from the Committee of Union and Progress in 1909 and felt free of the responsibility for the loss of the war.

The Allied occupation and partition of Turkey and the reduction of the Sultanic government to a mere puppet enraged many Turks. They were particularly incensed over the Greek landing (with Allied support) at Izmir

(May 14, 1919) and advance into the Anatolian interior.
In early 1919 the Sultan designated Mustafa Kemal as
Inspector General of the Third Army Headquarters in
Eastern Anatolia, with the assignment to supervise the
demobilization of Turkish forces in that part of Turkey
where there was resistance to Allied occupation. Two
army corps (six divisions) in the area were still under
arms. How it was that Mustafa Kemal was chosen for
this assignment remains obscure.

Mustafa Kemal found himself in the right place at the
right time. Among the resistance groups in the area was
the Eastern Anatolian Society for the Defense of National Rights. Here and elsewhere the people were divided, hungry, and exhausted from war. Mustafa Kemal
called for resistance to foreign occupation and succeeded in establishing a firm hold over the aforemen-
tioned society. For a time he went along with the Sultan,
operating on the assumption that the ruler was a captive
and unable effectively to represent the nation. It did not
take the Sultan long to recognize his enemy; he ordered
the arrest of Mustafa Kemal. But this could not be ac-
complished. In the meantime the Eastern Anatolian Society chose Mustafa Kemal as its chairman, and at a
Congress in Erzerum (July, 1919) adopted a resolution
for the defense of the integrity of national frontiers and
the convocation of the National Assembly. At the Congress of Sivas (September, 1919) the existing program
was spelled out and became the National Pact, calling
for a free and independent Turkey. A representative
committee was chosen, headed by Mustafa Kemal as
President.

The recent elections returned to the parliament in
Istanbul a Nationalist majority. The Nationalists were
condemned by the government and by the Sheykh ul-
Islam. In March, 1920, the British occupied Istanbul,
detained some of the Nationalists, and exiled others to
Anatolia, where they swelled the number of Kemalist
supporters. The Grand National Assembly, which met at
Ankara (April 23, 1920), was proclaimed the supreme
power of the state, and Mustafa Kemal was chosen its
President.

The Kemalists refused to accept the Treaty of Sèvres

(August, 1920), dictated by the Allies. They pressed against the Greeks, whom they decisively defeated at the Battle of Sakariya (August 26, 1922). They reached an agreement with the Soviet Union (March 16, 1921) and obtained military supplies from that country. They were also able to negotiate with other powers, and to secure advantages. By September 9 the Greeks were driven from Anatolia, and the Allies were obliged to negotiate a new armistice agreement with the Turks which provided for the removal of foreign troops from Anatolia and Eastern Thrace. Finally, on July 23, 1923, came the signing of the Treaty of Lausanne, the Turkish delegation being ably represented by Colonel Ismet Inönü, a distinguished soldier and the future president of Turkey.

In the meantime Mustafa Kemal had abolished the sultanate in 1922 on the grounds that the Sultan was a traitor to the country. On October 29, 1923, Turkey was proclaimed a Republic. As the new regime extended its sway over the country it encountered much opposition, but by March 3, 1924, the government was strong enough to abolish the caliphate headed by the descendant of the house of Osmanli. A constitution providing for a one-party totalitarian government was adopted on April 20, and Mustafa Kemal reorganized his followers into the ruling Republican Peoples' Party. Modern Turkey, founded on the principles of nationalism, secularism, étatism, and republicanism, became a stable and dynamic state, much healthier than the Ottoman Empire in its final days.

SUMMARY:
THE OTTOMAN LEGACY

Ottoman culture survived the Ottoman state. Both the Turks and their erstwhile subjects continue to exert a powerful influence drawn from their common heritage. Many consequences of Ottoman rule in the Near East are fundamental and enduring.

Islamization and Turkification. The large Muslim population in the Balkans, made up mostly of converted Christians, is a highly important ramification of the Ottoman legacy. Just which groups of the population most readily accepted Islam, the rate of Islamization and Turkification, and the means by which these processes operated has never been definitely determined. In the time of Ottoman rule most converts regarded themselves as Muslim Turks, whose customs they imitated without adopting their language. Nonetheless, a distinction was made between the minority of Turkish colonists and the majority of converted Muslims. Most of the Turkish colonists were settled in Macedonia, Bulgaria, Thrace, and the Dobrudja. Wherever the Turks made their home in the Balkans, they gave Turkish names to local places, translated the existing names into Turkish, or merely gave them Turkish speech forms.

During the long Ottoman rule Islam and Christianity influenced each other. Often Christian renegades retained their Christian religious customs. Some Christians called the object of their pilgrimage to the Holy Sepulchre in Jerusalem the *Ka'bah,* after the shrine in Mecca which is

116

the goal of the Muslim pilgrimage. Christian pilgrims received the appellation of *hajji* from the Arabic word for pilgrimage.

There are today in the Balkans, not counting Turkish territory, 2 million Muslim Albanians, 2 million Islamicized Slavs (Serbo-Croats, Macedonians, and Bulgarians*), about 400,000 original Turkish colonists, an estimated 150,000 Muslim Gypsies,* and insignificant numbers of other Muslim groups (Tatars, Circassians, etc.). After 1878 many well-to-do Muslims emigrated to Turkey, leaving the impoverished *rayah* behind.

The Resilience of Islam. Kemalism in Turkey and Communism in the Balkans have struck heavy blows at Islam, loosening its hold. The effects of secularizing policies on Muslim communities in Communist countries have been devastating. Many religious customs have been dropped, and the attendance in mosques has fallen. In the Arab countries Islam remains strong, even though it has lost some of its vitality, especially in the urban communities. Anatolian peasants still perform correctly the ceremonies of Islam and know a good deal about Muslim theology and tradition.

In Turkey during recent years Islam has manifested signs of revival. Attendance has been increasing in Turkish mosques. For a time Arabic texts appeared inscribed on the walls of coffee houses and shops. The Muslim press appears to be flourishing in Turkey. For the first time in many years Turks have resumed making pilgrimages to Mecca, and some Sufi brotherhoods (*tarikats*) have been reactivated.

Turkish Linguistic Influence. The Turks have left a lasting imprint on the languages of their subject peoples, and at the same time they themselves have taken over into their own vocabulary a large number of Arabic and other foreign words. The most impressive Turkish linguisitic influence occurred in the regions where Ottoman rule lasted the longest. Many of the surviving Turkish words in the languages of the subject peoples are administrative, legal, and economic terms left behind by

* The exact number is difficult to ascertain because some of them were expelled from Bulgaria to Turkey in the 1950's.

Ottoman officials, judges, and merchants. Turkish words employed by the Arabs consist mostly of political, administrative, and scientific terminology, usually formed out of Arabic roots.

Popular literature, especially the epic poetry which flourished during Ottoman rule, contains a mass of Turkish, Arabic, and Persian words. The milieu in which the poetry of the subject peoples developed and the events which inspired it required the use of Turkish terms, without which the poetry would have been like "food without spices." Some of the words were used only to embellish and flavor a sentence or stress a point. Many Turkish words became so much a part of the speech of the subject peoples that every attempt to expunge them from the written and spoken language has failed.

Often the words borrowed from the Turks represent things introduced by them, such as certain foods, fruits, beverages, vegetables, clothing and footwear, utensils and furnishings, musical instruments, construction materials, equine equipment, arms, crafts, commercial terms employed by artisans and merchants, and so on. Religious terminology, greetings, and personal names include a long list of Turkicisms still extensively used.

The Heritage in Literature. The Ottoman legacy in literature and folklore is likewise extensive. We have in mind particularly the Serbian epics, the Bulgarian *hayduk* ballads, the Greek songs of the *klephts*, the more recent Albanian songs (*kângë*), and the epics of the Yugoslav Muslims in Bosnia and Herzegovina, which depict the struggle of the local Muslims with the neighboring Christians. The most beautiful are the Serbian epics. Simple and lucid, they glorify individual and collective acts of heroism in the struggle against the Turks. These poems of decasyllabic lines center on some great historical event or a prominent personality. The Serbian poems, for example, describe the exploits of the legendary Kraljević Marko who at times cut down the Turks and at other times collaborated with them "for the benefit of the people." Details are given about the famous Battle of Kosovo (1389) in which King Lazar chose the "heavenly" kingdom in preference to the "worldly" and lost his life in defense of his followers. The epic poem helped the Christian peasant to preserve his ethnic individuality and his faith. While describing the almost unbearable life of the oppressed people the epics suggest plans for a future struggle against the Turks, who were depicted as tyrants ruling over the poor and weak.

The *hayduk* and *klepht* epics describe the exploits of brave men who took to the woods to wage guerilla warfare against the Turks. Although they were not always inspired by altruistic or patriotic motives, these men came to be regarded as Robin Hoods who suffered for the national cause and fought for the independence of themselves and their countrymen. As chronicles of past events and life under Ottoman rule, the epics are a rich source of historical and ethnographic information. While sometimes marked by exaggerations and flights of imagination, the epics record details of the religious and patriarchal life of the past.

Replete though the epic poems are with hate and prejudice, their destruction would mean the loss of a rich literary heritage. So significant is this problem in the contemporary lives of the Balkan peoples that in 1951 the Turkish and the Greek governments signed an agreement to "insure, within the limits permitted by respective legislation, that the textbooks published in the two countries do not contain inaccuracies relating to either of the two countries." But an agreement of this type can be enforced only with difficulty, for many a bright page in the history of one nation is a dark one in the history of the other. When the Turks* celebrated the five-hundredth anniversary of the conquest of Constantinople in 1953, the Greeks offered prayers in their churches to those who had fallen in defense of the city.

The Ottoman legacy will probably survive longest in literature, folklore, and ethnography. Among the most successful contemporary Balkan writers are those who deal with subjects drawn from the time of the Ottoman rule, such as Nikos Kazantzakis, the author of *The Greek Passion* (New York, 1954), and Yugoslavia's

* The Turkish government is said to have toned down somewhat the celebration so as not to offend the Greeks too much.

Nobel Prize-winning Ivo Andrić, who wrote the well-known *The Bridge on the Drina* (New York, 1959). The Christian-Muslim conflict is the main subject of both books.

Habits and Attitudes. The residuals of patriarchalism, perpetuated by Turkish rule, are still very much a part of the daily life of the Near Eastern peoples. The antiquated social system has helped to preserve primitive social practices and to mould a special set of human values. Under the Ottoman rule the Balkan peoples were reduced to a mass of illiterate peasantry who had known only the Turkish method of rule. The rebuilding of national states after centuries of Ottoman rule was for them an enormous problem.

Religious discrimination in the Ottoman Empire, coupled with constant exposure to a military atmosphere, produced particular spiritual traits in the subject peoples. The activities of the medieval *akritai,* who fought for the defense of Byzantine Christianity, and the *ghazis,* the Muslim warriors for the faith, and subsequently of the *klephts, hayduks,* and *uskoks,* created deep rifts between Christians and Muslims, and between peasants and landlords. The Ottoman social system fostered many undesirable habits (e.g., the bribe, or *bakhshish,* distrust of the government, and so forth) that lived on after the Empire's demise. Centuries of feudal bondage contributed to the prevalence of *yavashlik,* a state of being characterized by lethargy, indifference, indecision, and a tendency toward submissiveness which grew out of the necessity for survival. This can be easily detected in the attitude toward authority—apprehension but at the same time humility and acquiescence. Coupled with subservience is cleverness, expressed in attempts to get around obstacles, including those erected by authority, by using none-too-ethical (from the point of view of the government) or even illegal means. The notion persists that it is perfectly permissible to cheat and steal from the government, a problem with which none of the successor states has been able to cope altogether successfully. The peasant's suspicion of government, the police agent, and the tax collector has its origin, at least partially, in his experiences under Ottoman rule.

The future being uncertain, the subjects of the Ottoman Empire developed a rather hedonistic attitude toward life and a great appreciation of leisure. Work as
such is in general little prized by the Near Eastern
peoples; yet when transplanted from their own cultural
milieu to the United States, they find no difficulty in
acquiring industrious habits.

Many writers believe that fatalism (*kismet*), deeply
rooted in Balkan Christians, is a product of Islamic influence. Fatalism derives from the doctrine of predesti-
nation, namely, that everything has been ordained by
Allah or God and that no mortal can do anything to
change his destiny. The Christians, like their Muslim
neighbors, accepted the notion that upon everyone's forehead is written how long he will live!

Women. To some extent the Ottoman legacy is
also reflected in the treatment of women and children.
Although concubinage and certain other socially undesirable practices preceded the Ottoman conquest, there
was still a great difference between the status of women
in the medieval Balkans and the Byzantine Empire, on
the one hand, and their status in the Ottoman Empire,
on the other. In the former, women could ascend to the
throne and rule as queens and empresses; in the latter,
this was not possible. The Orthodox Church granted a
divorce to a woman on the grounds of desertion or
abandonment, but not so the Muslim judges. In many
parts of Turkey the right of women to secure a divorce
is not yet popularly recognized. The wife may, and sometimes does, leave her husband to return to her parents,
who usually re-admit her into the family fold.

The institutions of polygamy and the harem had a
degrading effect on women, who were generally treated
as inferior beings. Christian women for the most part
shared their fate, living in social isolation, deferring to
men with blind subservience, and in some districts adopting the veils and copying other articles worn by their
Muslim sisters. Until the Second World War one might
on occasion encounter an elderly Christian woman wearing the Muslim *dimije* (baggy trousers) in preference to
a modern skirt.

Since Islam still retains a powerful hold on Muslim

society, the emancipation of women has been slow. Women were left out of many religious activities; hence they knew little about religion or its doctrines and lore. The gulf created between man and woman has grown so wide that certain words and phrases are reserved for one sex or the other. In many a Near Eastern home the man still rules with absolute authority and his wife obeys him slavishly. As in Turkish Anatolia, a Christian woman in a Balkan village often eats apart with the children, and on trips she walks, laden with household goods, several steps behind her husband.

The segregation of women exists in Anatolia even today. The women may have friendly relations only with their close relatives, and must not be addressed by a stranger, nor can they address a stranger themselves. Every woman desires the birth of a son because he is a male. These and many other old social practices in connection with farming, stock-raising, births, funerals, and celebrations persist in Anatolian villages. Relationships between parents and children, husbands and wives, and older and younger members of a family are largely governed by the traditional social code. The family or clan (*kabile*) remains a potent force in many villages.

Rightly or wrongly, the treatment of children (especially females) with indifference and unkindness is also traced to Ottoman influence. Children are exploited in various occupations, particularly girls, who are likely to marry at an early age and thus become "someone else's fortune." Children, taught to serve their parents and to dedicate their lives to them, are subjected to iron discipline. Recent years, however, have produced changing attitudes toward both women and children. Again, Kemalism in Turkey and Communism in the Balkans have thoroughly undermined the traditional way of life.

The Coffee House. One of the most conspicuous gifts of the Ottomans to their subjects was the coffee house (*kahvehane*). This institution has survived the Empire and has expanded into parts of Europe never ruled by the Turks. The historian Ibrahim-i Pechevi says that until 1555 there were neither coffee nor coffee houses in Istanbul, and that in time everyone became addicted to coffee, including the *ulema,* the sheykhs, and the state officials. In spite of protests by religious and state authorities, the habit spread from Constantinople into the provinces. By the end of the sixteenth century even distant provincial cities had their *kahvehanes,* and the drinking of what some called the "Turkish poison" became extensive. The coffee houses served as social centers where the Muslims gathered to exchange gossip, tell stories, and discuss the political and religious issues of the day.

One still sees in many parts of the former Ottoman Empire *kahvehanes* packed with men of leisure. Not only are idle hours spent in the *kahvehane,* but dangerous thoughts germinate there. Whether it be a Greek *kaffeneion* or a Yugoslav *kafana,* the institution remains a gathering place for the men of the towns and villages, and it often serves as a village forum and place of entertainment. The *kahvehane* has become so much a part of Balkan life that not only its name but also a whole list of Turkish, Arabic, and Persian words centering about it have filtered into the native languages.

Food and Culinary Art. The Ottoman Turks left a lasting influence on the food and diet of the peoples they once ruled. The cuisine introduced or popularized by the Turks has survived in territories they once held. The antecedents of this cuisine, however, are subject to controversy. It is difficult to ascertain how much of the Ottoman menu is actually of Turkish origin. Patriots of nearly every ethnic group claim this dish or that as its own ancestoral invention. It is safe to assume that what foods the Turks did not originate, they popularized. Significance must be attached to the fact that many of the dishes and foods, including vegetables and fruit, have Turkish or Arabic or Persian names.

Thus, the Ottoman Empire gave the Near Eastern peoples not only a common historical experience, but much of their culture.

Part II

READINGS

— Reading No. 1 —

OTTOMAN EMPIRE AT ITS HEIGHT*

The Ottoman Empire had a long period of growing up, a relatively short span of maturity, and a protracted period of decline before its final doom. Ogier Ghiselin de Busbecq, imperial ambassador sent to negotiate with the Turks, left us an objective description of the Ottoman Empire at its height. He describes the Ottoman armed forces, which consisted of a wide variety of feudal and paid troops, each body with its own dress, symbols, and specific assignments. At the apogee of Ottoman power probably few armed forces match the Turks in combat effectiveness.

✓   ✓   ✓

The Sultan was seated on a very low ottoman, not more than a foot from the ground, which was covered with a quantity of costly rugs and cushions of exquisite workmanship; near him lay his bow and arrows. His air, as I said, was by no means gracious, and his face wore a stern, though dignified, expression. On entering we were separately conducted into the royal presence by the chamberlains, who grasped our arms. . . . After having gone through a pretense of kissing his hand, we were conducted backwards to the wall opposite his seat, care being taken that we should never turn our backs on him. The Sultan then listened to what I had to say; but the language I held was not at all to his taste, for the demands of his Majesty breathed a spirit of independence and dignity, . . . and so he made no answer beyond saying in a tetchy way, 'Giusel, giusel,' i.e., well, well. . . .

The Sultan's hall was crowded with people, among whom were several officers of high rank. Besides these there were

* *The Life and Letters of Ogier Ghiselin de Busbecq* (London, C. Kegan Paul and Co., 1881), Vol. I, pp. 152-156, 283-285.

all the troops of the Imperial guard, Spahis, Ghourebas, Ouloufedgis, and a large force of Janissaries; but there was not in all that great assembly a single man who owed his position to aught save his valour and his merit. No distinction is attached to birth among the Turks; the deference to be paid to a man is measured by the position he holds in the public service. There is no fighting for precedence; a man's place is marked out by the duties he discharges. In making his appointments the Sultan pays no regard to any pretensions on the score of wealth or rank, nor does he take into consideration recommendations of popularity; he considers each case on its own merits, and examines carefully into the character, ability, and disposition of the man whose promotion is in question. . . . Among the Turks, therefore, honours, high posts, and judgeships are the rewards of great ability and good service.

For the once, take your stand by my side, and look at the sea of turbaned heads, each wrapped in twisted folds of the whitest silk; look at those marvellously handsome dresses of every kind and every colour; time would fail me to tell how all around is glittering with gold, with silver, with purple, with silk, and with velvet; words cannot convey an adequate idea of that strange and wondrous sight; it was the most beautiful spectacle I ever saw.

With all this luxury great simplicity and economy are combined; every man's dress, whatever his position may be, is of the same pattern; no fringes or useless points are sewn on, as is the case with us, . . . They were quite as much surprised at our manner of dressing as we were at theirs. They use long robes reaching down to the ankles, which have a stately effect and add to the wearer's height, while our dress is so short and scanty that it leaves exposed to view more than is comely of the human shape; . . .

I was greatly struck with the silence and order that prevailed in this great crowd. There were no cries, no hum of voices, the usual accompaniments of a motley gathering, neither was there any jostling; without the slightest disturbance each man took his proper place according to his rank. The Agas, as they call their chiefs, were seated, to wit, generals, colonels (*bimbashi*), and captains (*soubashi*). Men of a lower position stood. The most interesting sight in this assembly was a body of several thousand Janissaries, who were drawn up in a long line apart from the rest; their array was so steady and motionless that, being at a little distance, it was some time before I could make up my mind as to whether they were human beings or statues; at last I received a hint to salute them, and saw all their heads bending at the same moment to return my bow. On leaving the assembly we had a fresh treat in the sight of the household cavalry returning to their quarters; the men were mounted on splendid horses, excellently groomed, and gorgeously accoutred. And so we left the royal presence, taking with us but little hope of successful issue to our embassy. . . .

I had the pleasure of seeing the magnificent column which was marching out. The Ghourebas and Ouloufedgis rode in double, and the Silihdars and Spahis in single file. The cavalry of the Imperial guard consists of these four regiments, each of which forms a distinct body, and has separate quarters. They are believed to amount to about 6,000 men, more or less. Besides these, I saw a large force, consisting of the household slaves belonging to the Sultan himself, the Pashas, and the other court dignitaries. The spectacle presented by a Turkish horseman is indeed magnificent. His high-bred steed generally comes from Cappadocia or Syria, and its trappings and saddle sparkle with gold and jewels in silver settings. The rider himself is resplendent in a dress of cloth of gold or silver, or else of silk or velvet. The very lowest of them is clothed in scarlet, violet, or blue robes of the finest cloth. Right and left hang two handsome cases, one of which holds his bow, and the other is full of painted arrows. Both of these cases are curiously wrought, and come from Babylon, as does also the targe, which is fitted to the left arm, and is proof only against arrows or the blows of mace or sword. In the right hand, unless he prefers to keep it disengaged, is a light spear, which is generally painted green. Round his waist is girt a jewelled scimitar, while a mace of steel hangs from his saddle-bow. . . . The covering they wear on the head is made of the whitest and lightest cotton cloth, in the middle of which rises a fluted peak of fine purple silk. It is a favorite fashion to ornament this headdress with black plumes.

When the cavalry had ridden past, they were followed by a long procession of Janissaries, but few of whom carried any arms except their regular weapon, the musket. They were dressed in uniforms of almost the same shape and colour, so that you might recognize them to be the slaves, . . . There is only one thing in which they are extravagant, viz., plumes, head-dresses, etc., and veterans who formed the rear guard were specially distinguished by ornaments of this kind. The plumes which they insert in their frontlets might well be mistaken for a walking forest. Then followed on horseback their captains and colonels, distinguished by the badges of their rank. Last of all rode their Aga by himself. Then succeeded the chief dignitaries of the Court, and among them the Pashas, and then the royal bodyguard, consisting of infantry, who wore a special uniform and carried bows ready strung, all of them being archers. Next came the Sultan's grooms leading a number of fine horses with handsome trappings for their master's use. He was mounted himself on a noble steed; . . . Behind him came three pages, one of whom carried a flask of water, another a cloak, and the third a box. These were followed by some eunuchs of the bed-chamber, and the procession was closed by a squadron of horse about two hundred strong.

— Reading No. 2 —

A VISIT TO THE SULTAN*

The extravagance of the Sultan's life, the beauty of the palace, and the pomp and ritual accompanying the official receptions impressed many European observers. Here are the observations by an American minister on his way to the palace to submit his credentials to the Sultan Abdul Hamid II.

✓   ✓   ✓

After crossing a spacious hall paved with marble, we are ushered into another reception-room. A large divan is at one end, and chairs all around the walls. The furniture is covered with red damask. In the middle of the room is a marble table. On this is placed a large silver candelabra for sixteen candles. Facing the divan is a pier-table supporting a large clock. This clock is of silver. Two magnificent Japanese vases are on each side. The floor is covered with a priceless Smyrna carpet. Everywhere—in palace or in mosque—the carpet plays a principal part in Turkey and in the East. . . . Then we proceed up a broad and elegant staircase in the following order: The American Minister is between the Minister of Foreign Affairs and the Grand Master of Ceremonies. . . . We now enter the audience-room. It is very wide and long.

* Samuel S. Cox, *Diversions of a Diplomat in Turkey* (New York: Charles L. Webster and Co., 1887), pp. 14-23.

Its floor is covered with a Turkish carpet. In the centre of the room is a long buhl table. There is a small table behind the Sultan, on which he leans while "audience" goes on. It gives him relief if the talks take too much dimension. The furniture in the room is not a prominent feature. Most of it is from Paris. The apartment receives light from three huge windows facing the east. On the walls hang superb oil paintings. . . . The Sultan receives us, standing on a rug made of camelhair felt, covered with embroidered flowers in different colored silk braid of Turkish work.

As we are ushered into the presence, we make three bows —one at the door on entering, the second half-way, and the last when we stop, a few feet from his person. We do not bow as low as the Turkish Ministers, but we do our best. The Sultan is standing at the far end of the room, in front of a table. As he is the conspicuous object of our attention, and a figure of great attraction, is it not proper to make a detailed description of this potentate of a great empire?

The Sultan is middle-sized and of the Turkish type. He wears a full black beard, is of dark complexion, and has very expressive eyes. His forehead is large, indicative of intellectual power. He is very gracious in his manner, though at times seemingly a little embarrassed. He is dressed in the uniform of chief marshal of the army. He wears the following decorations: The Grand Cordon of the Osmanli, which is a green scarf worn across the breast; the first class of the Medjidie, in diamonds; the Nichan Imtiaz, an order instituted by his grandfather, Sultan Mahmoud, and the Nichan Iftihar. The insignia and medals are inlaid with precious stones. The green sash or scarf is of a rich color and texture. No person was ever decorated in more gorgeous array, and yet in his bearing and demeanor he is unostentatious. Notwithstanding the prejudice of the Ottoman against images, his photograph has been permitted. The frontispiece, which represents him as a cavalier, is a faithful likeness.

There is an etiquette which Turkish officials observe in the Sultan's presence. It has been much modified by time, and since the Crimean War greatly modified, like other old habits here, especially as they affect strangers. On approaching the Sultan the officials, when about ten yards distant, make a salaam. This consists in bending the body till the right hand touches the ground. The hand is then brought to the heart, the mouth, and then to the forehead. What does this mean? Its idea is, that you take the earth from the ground as a symbol of lowliness. Then you carry the hand to your heart and head. The lips approve your regard. After the first salaam, you advance five or six yards and repeat. If you are an official, again and again you repeat until you are a yard and a half from the Sultan. Then a third salaam is made. Then the person stops. He crosses his hands on the lower part of his stomach. This is said to be a relic of Persian usage. It has a meaning. It is intended to show that the servant has no concealed weapon in his hand. These officials never address the Sultan. Every time he looks toward them they repeat the salaam. After much genuflexion they are asked what their business is. They tell their story and bow lowly and bow out.

On this occasion the Sultan had on his right, and standing in single file, with their backs to the wall, about fifteen of his most distinguished aides-de-camp. . . . The American Minister advances between the Foreign Minister and the First Chamberlain. . . . I receive the proper intimation, present my credentials, and speak the speech as it was set down, and with appropriate decorum. The hush of the place conquers my rhetoric. The low tones in which everybody speaks naturally reduces the compass of the voice. The speech is hardly two minutes' long, but after it is finished I am relieved. The Sultan is pleased to respond most amiably. He is pleased to say that he is gratified with the selection made by the President. He has great satisfaction in knowing that I had been in the country before, and was familiar with its affairs and government. He makes the usual reference to the happy relations always existing between the two nations, and expresses the hope that they would continue. He is glad to extend the same friendship to me that he extended to my predecessor. After some pleasant and informal talk, he steps forward and shakes me warmly by the hand. Then the guests are severally introduced to the Sultan, who expresses his gratification at having made their acquaintance. We then leave the room, walking backward, making three bows, as before. . . .

— Reading No. 3 —

A SULTAN'S FRIDAY VISIT TO THE MOSQUE*

The Sultan's traditional Friday visit to the mosque was the principal weekly spectacle in Istanbul, and it was always observed by large crowds who gathered for the occasion. The visit and the accompanying ceremonies lacked order and grandeur and were more remarkable as a military display than as a pageant. Below is an eye-witness account of a visit to a mosque by Abdul Hamid II.

✓   ✓   ✓

Every Friday in Constantinople is performed a ceremony called the "Selamlik" or public visit of the Sultan to a mosque for the mid-day prayer. Former sovereigns usually discharged this duty at St. Sophia or one of the principal religious edifices, in each of which is a Mahfil or Imperial pew. Abdul-Hamid II, however, has since the beginning of his reign shown a preference for the mosque in the immediate vicinity of Yildiz, and of late years has had one constructed for his special use, and to all intents and purposes in the palace grounds. From the gate of Yildiz descends a steep road bordered on one side by annexes of the palace, which terminate in two pavillions, one devoted to the reception of distinguished persons and ambassadors, while in the other are accommodated the common herd of sightseers. On the other side are a garden and a mosque, quite new, and unpretentious, but deriving a certain grace and dignity from the background, where the coast of Asia and Mount Olympus are seen rising from the Sea of Marmora.

Long before mid-day on Friday soldiers and spectators, among which latter are hundreds of Turkish women, occupy all the available space. Cohort after cohort of muscular peasants, drawn from every district of this variegated empire, marches up to the clang of barbarous music and takes

* Charles Eliot, *Turkey in Europe,* 2nd ed. (London: Edward Arnold Publishers, Ltd., 1908), pp. 110-115, 123-131, 138-139.

133

its place. As a military display the spectacle is remarkable; as a pageant, disappointing. Turkish ceremonies lack order and grandeur. Detectives thread their way through the crowd, and now and then arrest some poor innocent. Dirty-looking servants from the palace, wearing frockcoats, no collars, and white cotton gloves, hurry hither and thither, carrying dinners wrapped up in cloths, which are sent to various persons as complimentary presents from the Imperial kitchen. Fat men of great rank and girth drag about laboriously black Gladstone bags in which they brought uniforms stiff with gold. Tourists in strange headgear peep and gibber. Ultimately —for the Caliph avails himself of the letter of the law which says that the mid-day prayer must be said after the sun has begun to decline—ultimately a trumpet sounds. The troops salute and officials hastily confiscate the opera-glasses of the tourists, who are generally so surprised and indignant that they fail to notice what little they might have seen with their eyes. The trumpet sounds again, the soldiers shout "Long live our emperor!" and a victoria with the hood up comes slowly down the steep road.

On old man in uniform, Field-Marshal Osman Pasha, the hero of Plevna, sitting with his back to the horses, speaks with deep respect to some one seen less distinctly under the hood. The carriage stops at a flight of steps leading to the private door of the mosque. The hood is lowered by a spring, and he who sat beneath it alights, mounts the steps, and, in a moment of profound silence, turns and salutes the crowd. He has not come as the chief of a military race should come, on a prancing steed or with any dash and glory. There is no splendour in his dress or bearing; but for the moment that he stands there alone a solemnity falls over the scene, the mean and comic details disappear, and we are face to face with the spirit of a great nation and a great religion incarnate in one man.

Of all his subjects assembled there before him, there is not one whose life and fortune do not depend on his caprice; of all those wild men gathered together from Albania, Arabia, and the heart of Anatolia, there is not one but would fall down and kiss the hem of his garment did he deign address them, or cheerfully die to preserve his tyranny; of all those women, there is not one but would account his slightest and most transient favours her highest glory; of all those Liberals and Young Turks, there is not one who, when the time for talking is over and the time for action comes, will not submit to his will: for all that the Osmanlis can do, all they may suffer, all the ideas they can form of politics or statecraft are

centered in that one personality, and they who would depose
him can think of no better expedient than to appoint another
like him as his successor. . . .

— Reading No. 4 —

JANISSARIES *

*We still know very little about the origin, recruitment,
number, ritual, and organization of the Janissaries. The same
is true of the role they played in the military and political
life of the Ottoman Empire. Some sources exaggerate their
importance, while others contend that they were never a
substantial military force. The consensus, however, is that
until the sixteenth century the Janissaries were a closely knit
and powerful body of troops.*

       ✓   ✓   ✓

The distinctive feature of the janissary system is the recruitment of the corps from a levy of the Christian children
of the Empire, who were forcibly converted and specially
trained for their profession. It would appear . . . that . . .
the earlier Sultans maintained a kind of bodyguard or *corps
d'élite* formed of bought or captured slaves, who would
naturally be mainly Christians. This force was reorganized
after Orkhan's time, and the prisoners who composed it were
induced to become Muhammadans and undergo a thorough
military training. . . . That the levy of Christian children
was not yet (fifteenth century) systematized seems ob-
vious. . . .

Turning to the connexion of Haji Bektash with the janissaries, we gather that he was originally only a tribal saint
subsequently 'captured' and adopted by the Hurufi sect, who
foisted their own doctrines as those of Haji Bektash on the
latter's disciples. As the sect grew in power . . . Haji Bek-

* N. M. Penzer, *The Harem* (Philadelphia: J. B. Lippincott
  Company, n.d.), pp. 89-93.

tash was adopted as their patron, the connexion being officially recognized from 1591 onward. . . .

The recruits were obtained from all conquered countries, but mainly from Albania, Bosnia and Bulgaria. Their education and training followed immediately, the majority becoming *ajemoghlans* and doing hard manual labour to fit them for every type of physical endurance that might be necessary later on. The selected few were attached to the Palace School, and went through a complete system of education. Subsequently they would be put in command of some frontier garrison, and moved about from province to province as occasion demanded.

The laws were at first most strict, enforcing implicit obedience, absolute concord among the corps, abstinence from all forms of luxury, forbidding marriage or domestic ties of any kind, and demanding observance of all religious laws of Haji Bektash. Members of the corps were not to trade in any way, were to observe certain rules as to their toilet and dress, were not to leave their barracks, were to have no pay in peacetime, and were to receive arms only in time of war. Their rations were quite inadequate, and soon led to the breaking of some of the regulations. As time went on all kinds of abuses occurred, as we shall shortly see.

In 1551 Nicolay describes the janissary as being armed with a "scymitar, and a dagger with a little hatchet hanging at his girdle, using also long harquebusses which they can handle very well." Janissaries were not allowed to wear beards, but "to the intent they should seem the more cruel and furious in the aspect of their faces they let their mustachioes grow very long gross and thick." Their dress consisted of a dark blue cloth coat, while among the older members the Bektash headdress was enriched by an enormous plume of bird-of-paradise feathers, which fell in a curve down the back nearly to the knees. Nicolay gives a good drawing of this, as well as of the *Agha* (or Chief Commander) of Janissaries, with his embroidered under-coat, long hanging sleeves, and big turban. The colour of the boots at once proclaimed the rank of the wearer—red, yellow, and black in descending order being the colours worn.

The names of the officers were all connected with the culinary art. Thus the Agha was known as the *Chorbaji-bashi,* or Head Soup-distributor; then came the *Asci-bashi,* or Head Cook, followed by the *Sakka-bashi,* or Head Water-carrier. Their standard was emblazoned with a huge *kazan* ('kettle' or cauldron), which merits some detailed consideration. It is hard to say exactly when these 'kettles' began to play such an important part in the history of the corps. . . .

And so the 'kettles' came by degrees to be symbols of military pride, and, like our drums, were piled in the front of the tent of the *Agha* when the janissaries were in camp. On the march the 'kettles' were carried by recruits in relays, and their loss during a battle was a lasting disgrace to the *oda* of the *ocak*. The large regimental copper was borne by older men, and its loss was considered so grave that only some exploit of great daring could efface the stain. In times of peace the janissaries assembled in the Second Court after midday prayer every Friday to receive their due allowance of *pilaf*. The Sultan waited in the kiosk between the Divan and the Gate of Felicity, and watched the proceedings with considerable anxiety. If the 'kettle'-bearers fetched the rice from the kitchens at the accustomed signal all was well, but if they stayed in the ranks and turned the 'kettles' upside-down it was a symbol of dissatisfaction and possibly revolution. . . . The results were often terrible and swift; the *bostanji* would be summoned, the ringleaders and 'kettle'-bearers seized, and a pile of heads would soon appear outside the *Ortakapi*.

On the other hand, from the seventeenth century onward the power of the janissaries became tremendous, and not less than six Sultans were either dethroned or murdered through their agency. . . . So long, therefore, as [*the sultan*] led them into battle and retained the warlike spirit of the early sultans the military *morale* was maintained and the corps became the finest standing army in Europe.

But when the sultans exchanged the battlefield for the *harem* regulations became lax, the original spirit of the corps was neglected, and all kinds of abuses soon turned this fine body of men into the scourge and bane of the Ottoman Empire. Until the time of Murad III (1574) the number never exceeded 20,000 all told, but irregularities started in the middle of his reign, and by the end of the century the janissaries totaled over 48,000. This was due to several factors, all detrimental to the corps. No longer were the *odas* recruited only by the Christians, but by true Ottomans who had personal ties with the people, and no more did they look upon the Sultan as their father.

Long intervals of peace had stained the celibate janissaries with all kinds of vices and evil practices, and as soon as they felt their power growing they began to marry, and so became more independent than ever. If money or food was short a fire could easily be started, when wholesale looting would naturally follow. It is estimated that during the reign of Ahmed III (1703-1730) no less than 140 such fires occurred. The married janissaries were allowed to live out of barracks,

and soon not only their children, but friends and relations,
became enrolled as members of the corps.

Thus in time the percentage of utterly useless men and
downright scoundrels was very considerable, and early in
the nineteenth century the number on the payroll had reached
the enormous figure of over 130,000. . . .

— Reading No. 5 —

THE HAREM AND THE EUNUCH INSTITUTIONS *

*An integral part of the royal palace was the harem, which
was the sphere of the women and the eunuchs who guarded
them. The heart of the harem was the Sultan's family—his
wives, concubines, and children. The harem and the eunuch
institutions have existed in the Middle East and in the Far East
since very early times, and the Turks inherited them from
their precursors. Because of the powerful influence that they
at times had over the Sultans, the two institutions have received more attention from historians than they otherwise
might have. Yet, many points regarding the recruitment,
organization, and activities of the harem women and eunuchs
remain obscure. Few sources are as complete and as authori-
tative on the harem and eunuch institutions as the one from
which the following selections are taken.*

⸸   ⸸   ⸸

The female hierarchy of the *harem* was a complicated institution, having a definite and fixed number of officers, with
every woman occupying a distinct position according to her
age, status, and the point at which she had arrived in her
harem education.

The *harem*, then, must be regarded as a little kingdom of
its own, a curious kingdom certainly, but one in which there
was a ruler, the equivalent of a Prime Minister, a Cabinet,

* N. M. Penzer, *The Harem* (Philadelphia: J. B. Lippincott
Company, n.d.), pp. 134-135, 149, 174-176.

other less important officials connected with the governing, and finally the subjects—all occupying different positions, but all being given some definite job to do with a chance to improve their positions as time went on. Let us look at conditions as they were when the *harem* was at its height in the sixteenth and seventeenth centuries.

The ruler of the *harem* is not the Sultan, nor the head wife or First Kadin (recognized concubine), but the Sultan's mother, the Sultan Validé. The Turks recognized that a man can have many wives, that he can get rid of unwanted ones and take others at will, but that he can have only one mother, and it is she, therefore, who occupied the unique place of honour that nothing can alter save death. To her, then, are entrusted the most personal and private belongings of her son —his women. The power of the Sultan Validé is enormous, not only in the *harem,* but throughout the entire Empire. As is only to be imagined, there is ceaseless warfare between the Sultan's mother and his favourite *kadins.* The most ambitious woman in the *harem* is not she who is content to reach the high position of First Kadin, but she who hopes, plots, and prays to become one day the Sultan Validé; for then she is not merely ruler of the *harem* and of the Seraglio, but, if she is strong and her son weak, may even rule the kingdom as well.

No better example of the power and influence a member of the harem might acquire could be given than that of Khurrem, the Russian slave girl, better known in Western Europe as Roxelana. In this case, however, so great was her influence over Suleiman that the question of her becoming Sultan Validé never arose. Bit by bit Roxelana removed all obstacles in her path. About 1541 she had persuaded the Sultan to let her live with him in the Seraglio instead of remaining in the Old Palace, although at this time she was only Second Kadin. After the death of Suleiman's mother only two rivals remained—the First Kadin, Bosfor Sultan, and Ibrahim, the Grand Vizier, who according to some accounts had been the original owner of Roxelana. Plots and counter-plots were laid: Bosfor Sultan was displaced and practically exiled, her son was murdered in a manner that leaves little doubt as to Roxelana's complicity in the business, and Suleiman had the Grand Vizier executed for no apparent reason at all. Although no actual proof was forthcoming to show that Roxelana was again instrumental in this latter crime there is no doubt whatever that he was definitely in her way to absolute power, and she was still afraid of his great influence over the Sultan.

It had been a triumph when she was allowed to move into

the Seraglio with her train of slave girls and eunuchs; it was a much greater one when she became Suleiman's legal wife. Not since the time of Bayezid I (1389-1403) had any Sultan contracted a legal marriage, and this strange act of Suleiman was regarded with amazement and concern. . . .

In the event of the birth of a male child and the continued and growing affection of the Sultan a lucky *ikbal* might be raised to the coveted rank of a *kadin*. Although they were not actually married the rank of the *kadins* was equivalent to that of a legal wife, and their apartments, slaves, eunuchs, property, dresses, jewelry, and salary were all proportional to the honour and importance of their new positions. According to the order of her election, so would the *kadin* be henceforth known. Thus she might be the Second Kadin or Third Kadin, and naturally she would do all in her power to dislodge the one immediately above her—by fair means or foul. In the case of Roxelana, however, the impossible had been achieved, for Suleiman, so far from having other *kadins* after the fall of Bosfor Sultan, actually married off several of his most beautiful women to cement his affection and fidelity to Roxelana.

*   *   *

As time went on the Byzantine custom of the seclusion of majesty began to impress itself on the conquerors, and the methods previously employed to protect that majesty were also adopted, and so gradually the *harem* and the employment of eunuchs came into being. The two things went together as they always had done. Despotism and polygamy had created the necessity for eunuchs, and the injunctions of the *Koran* were overlooked with surprising rapidity and casualness. It was, of course, the swift development of the Turkish Empire that forced the pace. The continual victories . . . produced a rich booty in slaves. Presents of slaves, both male and female, from conquered emirs or princes wishing to gain the Sultan's favor and protection, would often include eunuchs, and once the innovation had proved a success the demand could easily be supplied.

Turkish historians date the introduction of the employment of eunuchs in the first quarter of the fifteenth century under Muhammad I and Murad II. This apparently refers only to white eunuchs. The black variety, however, were in use about 1475, while by the time of Suleiman the Magnificent Roxelana's personal guard consisted of both white and black eunuchs. With the moving of the royal *harem* from the *Eski Serai* to the new palace on Seraglio Hill about 1541 the institution became firmly established. As the power of the Ottoman Empire grew and the State coffers became full, so also the numbers in the Seraglio increased, and Court ceremony became even more elaborate than before. If formerly two eunuchs were sufficient to guard a door, now it was ten. And so the true Oriental love of pomp and display was given full rein, and the Greco-Byzantine splendour was revived once more.

But the reign of the eunuchs was a long one, and even in this twentieth century, in the time of Abd ul-Hamid II, their power was as great as ever. . . .

It will thus be realized that after adopting the Byzantine custom of employing eunuchs to guard their *harems* the Turks were very careful to use only those who were fully emasculated. White eunuchs—Georgians and Circassians— were given jobs that would never bring them into close touch with the women, as in most cases their castration was incomplete. . . .

— Reading No. 6 —

WHIRLING DERVISHES *

Despite a Koranic interdict against monasticism, there were very early manifestations of it in the Muslim world. Orders of dervishes appeared first in Central Asia and from there spread to Anatolia. There were thousands of dervishes in Turkey and at least 12 different orders. One of the largest and most celebrated was the Mevlevi order. The dervishes exercised powerful influence over particular groups (e.g., Bektashi influence on the Janissaries and the artisan guilds) with which they were associated. The dance (the mystical rite of the Mevlevi order) of the Whirling Dervishes, performed annually in the city of Konya, is a most beautiful spectacle. It is performed on the anniversary of the death of the Muslim poet and mystic, Mevlana Jelal ad-Din Rumi, who died in 1273. Kemal Atatürk suppressed all Dervish orders, but the annual festival of Konya has been permitted since 1947. Here is how one eyewitness describes it.

* The New York Times, January 19, 1964, p. 2, cols. 3-4.

Sixteen Dervishes wearing the traditional zikkes, tall hats that resemble elongated flower pots, and the black, voluminous gowns called the hirkas enter the arena, led by the Mevlevi Sheik. Their accompaniment is provided by an orchestra of about 20 musicians wearing Dervish garb.

The main instrument is the ney, a reed pipe originated in Persia, which has a long association with Islamic mysticism. There also is the rebab, a violin with one string, and the kudum, a kind of drum.

The music is repetitive and slightly hypnotic.

At first, the Dervishes sit motionless on the floor, their heads bowed in prayer or contemplation, while one of the musicians chants. Then comes a piercing solo from the ney, which seems to act like a summons. The Dervishes rise and, led by the Sheik, circle the arena three times in a halting gait.

After the third circle, the Dervishes throw off their black cloaks. Underneath the cloaks they are wearing flowing white robes with full skirts that reach almost to the ground. They are now ready for the Sema, or sacred dance.

One Dervish crosses his arms over his chest and hugs his shoulders. At the moment that he makes this gesture he begins, almost imperceptibly, to turn in a counterclockwise motion. The other Dervishes follow suit, gradually building momentum.

As they gather speed, their arms, as though propelled by centrifugal force rather than their own volition, unfold gradually to an outstretched position and so remain throughout the dance. The right palm faces upward, the left downward.

Some of the Dervishes spin rapidly, others rotate in a slower motion. There is order and apparently effortless precision throughout. The Dervishes' heads are inclined at a slight angle, their brilliant skirts flared by the motion.

A practiced Dervish can whirl, it is said, for an hour and a half without stopping.

As explained by the Mevlevi. Sheik, the symbolism is as follows:

The black cloaks symbolize the tomb, the tall hats tombstones. The white dancing robes represent the shroud.

At first, the Dervishes are unaware of divine power. Their halting gait is the walk of human life.

The casting off of the black gowns that follows represents the rising from the tomb. The hugging of the shoulders is a gesture of absolute surrender to the will of God.

The turning movement itself is the means by which mystical union can be achieved with God, the Mevlevi believe. The upturned right palm receives God's mercy from Heaven and transmits it through the downturned left palm to earth.

— Reading No. 7 —

TURKISH ART*

Turkish art has been a subject of much controversy. Some critics deny the Turks any real artistic originality and creativity. Others argue more persuasively that the Turkish art and architecture are syncretist, consisting of the artistic heritage of the Near East and the original Turkish art. After describing the beauty of some of the principal mosques in Istanbul, H. G. Dwight analyzes certain aspects of decorative art.

✓   ✓   ✓

Stamboul, indeed, is a museum of tiles that has never been adequately explored. Nor, in general, is very much known about Turkish ceramics. I suppose nothing definite will be known till the Turks themselves, or some one who can read their language, takes the trouble to look up the records of mosques and other public buildings. The splendid tiles of Suleiman's period have sometimes been attributed a Persian and sometimes a Rhodian origin—for they have many similarities with the famous Rhodian plates. The Turks themselves generally suppose that their tiles came from Kütahya, where a factory still produces work of an inferior kind. The truth lies between these various theories. That any number of the tiles of Constantinople came from Persia is impossible. So many of them could not have been safely brought so far overland, and it is inconceivable that they would have fitted into their places as they do, or that any number of buildings would have been erected to fit their tiles. The Rhodian theory is equally improbable, partly for similar reasons though chiefly because the legend of Rhodes is all but exploded. . . .

That tiles were produced in Asia Minor long before the capture of Constantinople we know from the monuments of Broussa, Konia, and other places. They were quite a different kind of tile, to be sure, of only one colour or containing a

* H. G. Dwight, *Constantinople Old and New* (New York: Harper & Brothers, 1915), pp. 42-55.

143

simple arabesque design, which was varied by a sort of tile
mosaic. Many of them, too, were six-sided. The only examples
of these older tiles in Constantinople are to be seen at the
Chinili Kyöshk of the imperial museum—the Tile and the
tomb of Mahmoud Pasha. It is a notorious fact, however,
that the sultans who fought against the Persians brought back
craftsmen of all kinds from that country and settled them in
different parts of the empire. Selim I, for instance, when he
captured Tabriz, imported the best tile makers of that city,
as well as from Ardebil and Kashan—whence one of the
words for tiles, *kyashi*—and settled them in Isnik. . . .

The art itself declined and gradually died out as the sultans
stopped making conquests and building mosques. For the
imperial mosques are monuments of victory, built and en-
dowed out of the spoils of war. After the martial period of
the empire came to an end with Suleiman I only one mosque
of importance, that of Ahmed I, was built by a reigning sultan
in his own name. But the tiles of the imperial factories, after
many fires and much thieving, still make up what is most
brilliant and most durable in the colour of Stamboul. The
best tiles are Nicene of the sixteenth century, that extraordinary *cinque-cento,* when so many of the best things of the
world were produced. They are distinguished by the trans-
parent white glaze of their background, on which are drawn
tulips, carnations, wild hyacinths, and a certain long bent
serrated leaf common to the Rhodin plate. The chief colours
are a dark and a turquoise blue and a tomato red, green and
yellow occurring more rarely. And they are never quite
smooth, the red in particular usually being in slight relief.
This gives them a variety which is absent from many modern
tiles.

The feeling for variety, in fact, was one great secret of
Turkish tile making and tile setting. Sinan, for instance, used
tiles very sparingly in his larger buildings. He was great
enough to depend very little on ornament for his effect, and
he knew that tiles would look like paper or linoleum—if
such things existed in his day!—on a monumental surface.
But he had a perfect tact of using this tapestry wherever he
wanted a touch of colour or distinction—over a window,
along a cornice, around a *mihrab*. His masterpiece in this
decoration is the mosque of Rüstem Pasha, son-in-law and
Grand Vizier to Süleiman the Magnificent. This mosque,
lifted on retaining walls above the noise of its busy quarter,
has a portico which must have been magnificently tiled—
judging from the panel at the left of the main door—and
the whole interior is tiled to the spring of the dome. The

mosque is small enough for the effect of the tiles to tell—
and to be almost ruined by the fearful modern frescoes of
the vaulting. . . .

Two mosques of a later period in Stamboul are completely
tiled, that of Sultan Ahmed I and the one begun by his wife
—Yeni Jami. They prove the wisdom of Sinan in not at-
tempting to tile a large interior. Still, the gallery of Sultan
Ahmed also proves that the architect was not altogether
ignorant of what he was about. He put his best tiles there,
where they can only be seen at close range. And his best is
very good. I have counted twenty-nine varieties of tiles there,
or rather of designs, divided, like those of Rüstem Pasha,
into framed panels. The tiles facing the *mihrab,* where the
gallery widens over the main doorway, are so good that I
sometimes ask myself if the architect did not borrow from
an earlier building. Two series of eleven panels, one above
the other, make a tall wainscot whose only fault is that too
much richness is crowded into too narrow a space. The
lower series is the finer. Five panels to the right balance five
panels to the left of a spindle-shaped Persian design. Its
two neighbours are conventionalised cypress trees, than which
nothing more decorative was ever invented. Then come two
magnificent panels of larger spindles against a thicket of
peach-blossoms or Judas blossoms, red with small blue centres, followed by two more cypresses. Five panels of the upper
series, one of them forming the axis, are latticed again with
blossoming sprays. In this case there is no spindle to hide
the greater part of the flowers, which are blue with small
red centres. The tiles are very nearly if not quite as good
as those of the preceding century, and they make a wall
more splendid than exists outside the old Seraglio.

Yeni Jami is better suited for tiling, being comparatively
a smaller mosque. Its proportions are also much better and
the frescoing is not so bad as that of Sultan Ahmed. The
tiles themselves are not so interesting. But attached to the
mosque, and giving entrance to the imperial tribune, is a
suite of rooms which are also tiled. This imperial apartment
is carried across the street on a great pointed arch, and is
reached from outside by a covered inclined way which enabled the Sultan to ride directly up to the level of his gallery.
At the same level is also a little garden, held up by a massive
retaining wall, and a balcony with a rail of perforated marble once gave a magnificent view over the harbour. The
view has since been cut off by shops, and the apartment
itself has fallen into a sad state of neglect or has been subjected to unfortunate restorations. A later and more intelligent restoration has brought to light, under a vandal coat of

brown paint, the old gilding of the woodwork. But the tiles of the walls remain—except where they have been replaced by horrible panels of some composition imitating Florentine mosaic. Among them are charming cypresses and peachtrees. There are also remains of lovely old windows, to say nothing of tall hooded fireplaces and doors incrusted with tortoise-shell and mother-of-pearl. The tiles are palpably of a poorer period than those I have described. But there is a great attractiveness about this quaint apartment, that only adds to the general distinction of Yeni Jami.

— Reading No. 8 —

TURKISH POETRY*

Widely respected by contemporaries and probably the greatest Turkish poet and man of learning was Muhammad Baki (1527-1600), who wrote several excellent works under the influence of Persian lyrics. His best creations are the ode to his friend and patron Sultan Suleiman the Magnificent upon his return from the Persian campaign in 1555 and the well-known elegy dedicated to the memory of the same Sultan, whose death in 1566 he took as a great loss. The translation of the elegy, which follows, was done by Bernard Lewis.

✓   ✓   ✓

Oh you, whose foot is caught in the snare of fame and glory,
How long will you covet the things of this restless world?

Think of that day when, at the end of the spring of life,
The tulip-coloured face will turn into an autumn leaf.

For you, as for the dregs in the cup, earth must be the last
    dwelling;
The stone from the hand of time must strike the cup of life.

He is a man indeed whose heart is clear as a mirror.
If you are a man, why should the tiger's spite be in your
    breast?

* From *Istanbul and the Civilization of the Ottoman Empire*, by Bernard Lewis. Copyright 1963 by the University of Oklahoma Press.

Till when will the sleep of neglect lie on the eye of experience?
Are you not content with what has befallen the emperor, the
    lion of war?

That master-rider of the realm of bliss
For whose careering steed the field of the world was narrow.

The infidels of Hungary bowed their heads to the temper of
    his blade,
The Frank admired the grain of his sword.

He laid his face to the ground, graciously, like a fresh rose
    petal,
The treasurer of time put him in the coffer, like a jewel.

*   *   *

The day is born. Will not the lord of the world
    awake from sleep?
Does he not show himself from his pavilion,
    that is like the heavens?

Our eyes are on the roads, no word has come
From the place where lies the dust beneath the threshold
    of his majesty.

The colour of his cheek has gone, he lies dry-lipped
Like a fallen rose apart from the rose water.

Sometimes the Emperor of the skies hides behind the
    curtain of cloud,
When he remembers your grace he sweats with shame
    from the cloud.

This is my prayer: all those who do not weep for you,
Young and old, may their tears be buried in the ground.

May the sun burn and blaze with the fire of your parting;
In grief for you, let him dress in black weeds of cloud.

Weeping tears of blood as it recalls your skill,
May your sword plunge into the ground from its scabbard.

May the pen tear its collar in grief for you,
The standard rend its shirt in affliction.

— Reading No. 9 —

THE PALACE SCHOOL*

Until the nineteenth century Ottoman education was exclusively in the hands of religious leaders and teachers, and was conducted in conformity with Islam and its traditions. There were no higher schools, no institutions comparable to Western universities, and only a few secondary schools. The most famous of the Ottoman secondary institutions of learning were the Palace School and its various affiliates, founded by Mehmed II for the education of "valiant soldier and scholarly official" needed to serve the empire.

✔   ✔   ✔

Under Muhammad's enlightened direction the Palace School expanded and took on the definite character of a school of government, and so perfect an instrument did it prove for the purpose for which it was designed that its perpetuation and development became one of the most conscious policies and most powerful traditions of his successors. Primarily and essentially secular in its purpose . . . the Palace School of the Turkish sultans was a greater departure from the theological or *medreseh* type of education than the medieval university was from the monastic and cathedral schools.

. . . Besides the "two permanent teachers" resident in the Grand Seraglio . . . the nucleus of the faculty must almost certainly have been the dozen or more royal preceptors drawn from among the various ranks of the Ulema attached to the *medresehs* in the city, and from among the numerous savants whom Muhammad had gathered about himself from every point of the compass, veritably converting his palace, as Ata says, into a school (*mekteb*). Usually these preceptors were doctors of law (*mullahs*) and among the most

* Reprinted by permission of the publishers from *The Palace School of Muhammad the Conqueror,* by Barnette Miller (Cambridge, Mass.; Harvard University Press, Copyright, 1941, by the President and Fellows of Harvard College), pp. 31-34, 94-96, 126-127.

148

distinguished members of the Ulema, corresponding to the bishops of the palace school of Charlemagne.

But it is especially noteworthy that, within the fraternity of learning and letters resident at Muhammad's court, there were to be found Christians as well as Moslems, among whom were a number of Greeks. A recent Turkish biographer of Muhammad, Namiq Kemal Bey, says that, following the conquest of Constantinople, Muhammad made a great effort to stop the flight to Italy of Greek scholars, writers, teachers, philosophers, and men of letters in general, and to retain as many as possible in the capital, and that he employed Greek scribes for the purpose of diplomatic correspondence with Venice, Genoa, and Rhodes, and also as official chroniclers, a custom that was continued until the reign of Selim II.

Among the more notable Greeks who were attached to the court of Muhammad was the historian Critoboulos, who entered the Turkish service about the time of the conquest of Constantinople. He was later governor of Imbros until it was occupied by the Venetians in 1466, after which it is probable that he went to Constantinople. He wrote a life of Muhammad II, which for its accuracy and intimate acquaintance with the affairs of the court is reckoned one of the most valuable of the period. The Greek whose work is less known than that of Critoboulos . . . was the philosopher George Amyrutzes, who accompanied the Emperor David Paleologus to Constantinople after the fall of Trebizond, shortly thereafter "turning Turk with all his children, and receiving great employment in the Seraglio." A high authority on the systems of the Peripatetics and the Stoics, he is said to have been equally well versed in mathematics, physics, rhetoric, and poetics. . . .

The type of governing official which the Turkish sultans desired to produce through the medium of their palace system of education was the warrior-statesman and loyal Moslem who, at the same time, should be "a man of letters and a gentleman of polished speech, profound courtesy, and honest morals." To this end a student of the Palace School, from the day of his admission until he quitted the Grand Seraglio, was meticulously drilled in the ceremonies of the Moslem religion and Turkish etiquette. A contemporary judgment bears witness to the effectiveness of this social training: "The Turkish nobles, pages, people of the court and palace are reared in a politeness which excels the politeness and urbanity of other nations." The pages received instruction also, in almost equal proportions, in the liberal arts, in the art of war and physical exercise, and in vocational training—a

combination which seems to have been paralleled only by
the samurai, the warrior-scholars of Japan.

The liberal arts, in the Turkish, or Islamic, interpretation
of the term, embraced the Turkish, Arabic, and Persian
languages; Turkish and Persian literatures; Arabic grammar
and syntax; a study of the Koran and leading commentaries
upon it; Moslem theology, jurisprudence, and law; and Turkish history, music and mathematics. Of the last subject the
only branch which is known with certainty to have been
taught in the palace schools is arithmetic, although it seems
likely that instruction may also have been given in geometry.
The great Turkish architect of the sixteenth century, Sinan
Bey, who was educated in one of the Janizary barracks in
Constantinople, probably that in the Hippodrome, almost
certainly received some instruction in geometry as preparation for his later work as an engineer, and it is a well-
established fact that the curriculum of the Palace School
was much more comprehensive and advanced than that provided for the Janizaries. . . .

The nine palace schools—five preparatory schools and
four vocational schools—formed a closely correlated system
of education. At the same time each of the schools was a
separate and self-subsisting unit. As has already been stated,
the three outside, or auxiliary schools of Adrianople, Galata
Saray, and Ibrahim Pasha, were preparatory schools for the
Great and Small halls, while these two halls were in turn
preparatory to the three vocational schools, the halls of the
Expeditionary Force, or the Commissariat, and of the Treasury. . . .

During the period when the Palace School was at its height,
the full course of training extended over an average period
of fourteen years. After serving a novitiate of seven or eight
years in any one of the auxiliary schools, the pages were
promoted to either the Great Hall or the Small Hall, or else
were permitted to leave the auxiliary schools with the rank
of *Sipahis* of the reserve corps. As the number of students
in each of the four vocational schools was small and rigidly
limited, only a relatively small proportion of those who entered the preparatory schools were promoted to any one of
the schools of vocational training, and a still smaller proportion completed the entire course, the majority being sent out
to inferior posts in the army and government upon the com-
pletion of the preparatory school course. The curriculum of
each school was therefore carefully planned, not only with
a view to promotion from one school to another in hierarchi-
cal order but equally with a view to appointment to military
and civilian posts of corresponding grade. . . .

— Reading No. 10 —

DECLINE OF THE OTTOMAN EMPIRE *

The causes of the Ottoman decline are many, and interpretations are varied. Some historians see the seeds of decay embedded in the basic structure of the Ottoman Empire because it was organized primarily for warfare, covered a far-flung and unwieldy area, inhabited by heterogeneous population culturally and economically unevenly developed, and because of lines deliberately drawn between Muslims and Christians. Others find the reasons for the fall of the Ottoman Empire in the external pressures and economic and social crises after the sixteenth century. Specifically they refer to the breakdown in the apparatus of government, the decline of the armed forces, the halting of Ottoman advance in Europe, the circumnavigation of Africa, and the flow of precious metals from America. By the eighteenth century the Ottoman empire was in a state of rapid decay, and this was, as the statement below shows, apparent to any intelligent observer.

✓   ✓   ✓

If the Ottoman Empire is still vast and extensive; . . . [*nonetheless*] in the enervating lap of sloth, the ferocious conqueror has degenerated into a torpid barbarian, whose only marks of former prowess are to be traced in the insolence of his present demeanour, and the fallen affection of his fancied dignity. . . .

The relaxation of the bands of power has gone too far in the Turkish empire not to be, in some degree, perceived by the porte; it cannot but feel the weakness of his authority over most of the distant pashaliks. . . .

Casting our view over the pashaliks or governments most immediately connected with the feat of empire, we shall find them distracted, and scarcely yielding more than a nominal obedience to the sultan: such are the pashaliks of Asia Minor and Syria. With regard to the more distant provinces,

---

* William Eton, *A Survey of the Turkish Empire,* 4th ed. (T. Cadell and W. Davies, London: 1809), pp. 126-127, 275, 278-281, 284.

they may be considered as connected with the porte rather by treaty than as integral parts of the empire. In this light I view Moldavia and Wallachia on the north, and Egypt on the south. These unfortunate countries . . . suffer, though in different degrees, from the harpy touch of Turkish despotism. . . .

The great pashalik of Bagdad has been in reality independent, except at very short intervals, ever since the days of Achmet Pasha, who defended it against Nadir Shah, the famous usurper of Persia. The Sultan only confirms the pasha, whom the people, and principally the soldiery of Bagdad, have appointed to govern them with despotic power; the firman, however, sent on these occasions, always mentions the pasha as being nominated by the sublime porte to this high and trusty office, in consideration of his virtues, and some signal service he has rendered to the empire; and this farce is kept up by a new firman sent every year to continue him in office, as if the porte really had the power to remove him.

The porte draws no revenue from this extensive province.

The pasha, who has always a large army in his pay, and entirely devoted to him, sends regularly an account of the revenue of his government. This he always proves is totally absorbed by the expenses of the army, which he states as necessary to be kept on a formidable footing, to serve the empire against any attacks of the Persians or Arabs, and by the reparation of fortresses, that formerly existed, and of which no vestige now remains, etc. Whenever there is a war with an European power, and the pasha of Bagdad is called on to furnish his quota of troops, he pretends the necessity of keeping them all at home, to defend the province against the attacks of the Arabs, and finds means to provoke some Arab nation on the banks of the Euphrates, carries on a sham war. In short, the sultan is the nominal sovereign of Bagdad, but the pasha has the real sovereign independent power in his hands.

In Armenia Major, and all the neighboring countries, there are whole nations or tribes of independent people, who do not even acknowledge the porte, or any of its pashas. The three Arabias do not acknowledge the sovereignty of the sultan, who only possesses, in these countries a few unimportant towns. The pasha of Ahiska cares very little for the porte; and the famous Haggi-Alli-Yenikli-Pasha of Trabisonde, was the master of all that country; he could bring a large army into the field, and often set the porte at defiance. In the country about Smyrna, there are great *agas,* who are independent lords, and maintain armies, and often lay that city under contribution. The porte never gains but a temporary influence, by sometimes intermeddling in their quarrels.

All the inhabitants of the mountains, from Smyrna to Palestine are perfectly independent, and are considered by the porte as enemies, whom they attack whenever there is an opportunity. They are composed of different nations, who have their own sovereigns or lords, and are even of different religions. Those near Smyrna are Mahomedans; farther down come the Curdes, a very ferocious and faithless people. In the neighborhood of Aleppo there are various sects of religion. The mountains of Antilibanus are inhabited by Druses and Christians, and have, at times, been formidable to the Porte; they have more than once taken Damascus, and plundered it. . . .

All Egypt is independent. The pasha sent to Cairo is in effect a prisoner during his government, which is only nominal; the porte draws little or no revenue from it, and no troops, except a few fanatics in time of war with the Christians. The Turks have at different times got possession of Cairo, but never could maintain themselves in the government. The last instance of their subjecting the capital was by the late Hassan, captain pasha, but it was soon lost again; yet Constantinople depends very much on Egypt for provisions, and above all for rice. The Russians, when they had a fleet in the Mediterranean, very much distressed the porte, by cutting off the communication with Egypt, and might have done it much more, had they not permitted many neutral vessels to supply them.

In Europe, the Morea, Albania, Epirus, and Scutari, are more or less in a state of rebellion; Bosnia, Croatia, etc. obey the porte only as long as it suits them, and the sultan reaps little benefit from them. These latter countries afford the most robust and warlike soldiers in the empire; they are accustomed to arms from their infancy, as they are continually fighting among themselves, district against district, and often even village against village, besides individual quarrels of families. . . .

Lately we have seen almost all European Turkey in arms against the porte, Adrianople in imminent danger, and even Constantinople itself trembling for its safety.

— Reading No. 11 —

KLEPHTS AND ARMATOLI*

Throughout the history of the Ottoman Empire various bands either fought the established order or engaged in plunder as a means of livelihood. There were Muslim and non-Muslim bands. The Christian bands in the Balkans acquired the character of national movements against the Ottoman oppression. This is how they are remembered in the historical annals and epic poetry. The best known of the bands are the Greek klephts *and the Serbian and Bulgarian* hayduks (*from Turkish* haydut). *The following passage describes the role of the* klephts (clefts) *in modern history.*

✦   ✦   ✦

We have already seen that when the rest of the mountaineers submitted to the Turkish power, a certain number preferred to remain as outlaws in the mountain strongholds, and to maintain their independence in a wild life surrounded by privations. Accordingly the name of Cleft, or robber, which they received signified something very different from ordinary brigands, as it was only the conquerors and oppressors of their brethren who were the objects of their animosity and their marauding expeditions; and with the subject race they usually maintained a good understanding, and were regarded as the assertors of their liberties in time of need. But in the course of time this name obtained a wider signification in the following manner. As long as the rights of the Armatoles†

* Rev. Henry Fanshawe Tozer, *Researches in the Highlands of Turkey* (London: John Murray, Albemarle Street, 1869), Vol. II, pp. 46-57.

† Applied to a local militia, or rural police, composed entirely of native Christians, to whom was entrusted in great measure the security of the country where they were established. The institution extended over the greater part of those provinces of Turkey which were occupied by a Greek population, from the banks of the Vardar, towards the north, to the gulf of Corinth to the south, including also Epirus, Aetolia, and Acarnania. These were divided into districts, varying in number at

were respected by the Turks, they served, as we have said, to maintain order throughout the country: but as soon as they were attacked and forced to stand on the defensive, their character was at once changed, and they assumed the attitude of hostility which they had originally taken up against the conquerors. In this way they for the time became Clefts, and both received this title from others and acknowledged it themselves. When peaceful relations were re-established, they resumed their service as Armatoles; but at last the change from one character to the other was made so suddenly and so rapidly, that the two names came to be regarded as interchangeable, and sometimes those who were living in defiance of the Government were called Armatoles, and sometimes those who were peacefully engaged in maintaining order were called Clefts.

The most famous among all the headquarters of these bands was Mount Olympus. In that neighborhood they continued to exist as late as 1830, when Mr. Urquahart visited the country; and the account which he has given of the captain of a band of Armatoles presents a lively picture of the patriarchal authority of these officers, and their summary mode of administering justice. In the ballads the Clefts of Olympus are constantly mentioned. From the heights of that mountain they are described as watching the Albanians who are in pursuit of them below, and its deep gorges afforded excellent hiding-places, or *lemeria,* . . . which formed the *rendezvous* of the band during the day; while at night, when there was no need of concealment, they either slept in the open air, or sallied forth on some predatory excursion. . . .

As a general rule, it was only the Turks who suffered from the attacks of the Clefts. They were considered their rightful prey, and were constantly the object of their incursions, sometimes their villages and farms being burnt, while at others the rich owners were themselves carried off to the *lemeri,* and detained there until a sufficient ransom had been paid. But when the robber bands were reduced to extremities, they used also to plunder the wealthier of their own country men who dwelt in the plains, especially the bishops, whom they regarded as agents of the Turks. Thus it is that in some of the ballads we hear of persons called

different times, in each of which a separate body of Armatoles was organised, with a captain of its own, whose office was hereditary. The individuals who composed these bodies commonly called themselves Palicars, and wore the dress and arms of an Albanian soldier; the captain was styled Protopalicar.

Charamides, that is, brigands and murderers, who inspired the greatest terror into the merchants and owners of property. . . .

The shepherds especially are spoken of as the close allies of the Clefts. In this respect they are to be wholly distinguished from the ordinary brigands of the present day, who are the terror and aversion of the people at large. And notwithstanding the acts of violence which at times they did not scruple to commit, they seem to have been usually humane and generous, especially in their treatment of women, who were always safe in their hands, whatever their race or creed. Nor did they ever indulge in those barbarous cruelties which the Turkish Pashas were wont to practice towards any of their number who were taken prisoners. To all this must be added, in explanation of their great popularity, the fame of their extraordinary prowess, skill, and endurance. Their accuracy as marksmen, whether in ordinary mountain warfare by day, or in noting the position of an enemy by the flash of his gun by night; their wonderful strength and agility, arising from their wild life in the open air, and the gymnastic exercises to which their leisure hours were devoted; their power of supporting hunger, thirst, and want of sleep during successive days and nights of combat; and the courage with which they faced death and endured the horrible tortures to which they were exposed as prisoners,—all tended to make them objects of enthusiastic admiration to their countrymen. When the winter arrived, and the mountains were no longer habitable on account of the cold, the Cleft concealed his arms in the *lemeri,* and descended to the lowlands, where he took refuge either in some safe hiding-place on the mainland, or, as was more commonly the case, in the Ionian Islands, which at that time were subject to Venice. But wherever he appeared, he attracted attention and curiosity as one who had defied the common enemy, and slain a multitude of foes. His praises were celebrated in numerous ballads, which circulated from mouth to mouth among the people. Even the children in their games used to play at Turks and Clefts, dividing themselves into two bands, to represent the two opposing parties. . . .

— Reading No. 12 —

TURKISH EDUCATION IN THE NINETEENTH CENTURY*

Since the beginning of the eighteenth century the Turks had discussed reforms in education. In the second half of that century military schools were founded and modern scientific subjects taught. The nineteenth century ushered in more extensive reforms, involving both military and civil education. But the old traditionalist schools were not replaced by new. This dichotomy did not serve the imperial cause while at the same time the debates over the pedagogical methods and secular versus Muslim education continued unabated.

✓   ✓   ✓

Here I shall not discuss the history of education in Islam, but rather present-day problems. In other words, I shall try to show that the religion of Islam is one of our ideals in education.

If we study the curriculum of a [*Turkish*] school, we notice that [*Turkish*] children are taught according to three categories of learning: (1) They are taught language, literature, and history, which are Turkish language, literature, and history; (2) they are educated in the Kur'an, *tecvit* [*reading the Kur'an with the proper rhythm and pronunciation*], catechism, and the history of Islam and Islamic languages [*Arabic and Persian*]; (3) they are also trained in mathematics, natural sciences, and foreign [*European*] languages, which will aid them in their further studies in these sciences, as well as such skills as handicrafts and gymnastics.

This shows that the aims we pursue in our education are three; Turkism, Islamism, and Modernism. No Turkish father can fail to have his child educated in the Turkish language or allow him to remain ignorant of Turkish history. Also he cannot let him be ignorant of Islamic beliefs and rituals, or unacquainted with the history of Islam. But he

* Ziya Gökalp, *Turkish Nationalism and Western Civilization,* translated and edited by Niyazi Berkes (New York: Columbia University Press, 1959), pp. 233-235.

also wants his child to be trained as a modern man, in addition to his education as a Turk and a Muslim. It seems, therefore, that complete education for us would comprise three fields; Turkish education, Islamic education, and modern education.

Before the *Tanzimat,* Turkish children were educated solely in Islamic studies. Reforms of the *Tanzimat* period tried to introduce secular education. At first, there were grave conflicts between religious and secular education. Instruction in drawing and the French language met with strong opposition when introduced into secular schools. It was claimed that teaching the roundness of the earth or the heliocentric system was contrary to dogma, and it became necessary to seek evidence in dogma to support the truths which have been proven by observation and reason. However, with the passage of time, secular education gradually became established and rooted. But, unfortunately, the more secular education gained prestige, the more Islamic education lost its importance. It is true that religious instruction in the [*secular*] school curricula continued to occupy an important place. But the decline seen in Islamic education was in quality rather than in quantity: Religious instruction lost its vitality. Teachers of religion continued to look down on the sciences as objectionable upstarts (*bid'at*), and thus lost their prestige in the eyes of the students. Moreover, the application of scientific educational methods to this religious education had not ever been started.

. . . But not only did we fail to give our children a Turkish and Islamic education, we also did not succeed in giving them a modern education. However, it is modern education which might have enabled our children to make and use the technical instruments which are produced and used by advanced nations. By our failures, we proved that we were incapable of using modern techniques in military as well as in economic spheres. The test of science is action. By our failures in action we demonstrated our ignorance in sciences. Thus, both our institutions of higher learning, which should have trained specialized scientists, and our colleges, which should have educated citizens, did not achieve their aims.

At the present time, three groups of intellectuals are trying to lay the foundations of a new education. On the one hand, Turkish pedagogues are pointing out the important role that national traditions should play; the modernist pedagogues, on the other hand, are showing new methods to be applied in education based on the idea of the practical and economic applications of .modern science. In the third place, however, it is also necessary to discover the foundations upon which a new Islamic education may be based.

These three aspects of education must aid and complement each other. But if we fail to define the function and delimit the sphere of each in a reasonable way without overstressing any one of them, they may be contradictory and even hostile to each other. When secular education transgresses its own material realm and reaches into the spiritual realm, it clashes with the education of Turkish and Islamic ideals. To distinguish the boundaries between national and religious education, on the other hand, is more difficult. It requires extensive studies to show which of the Islamic traditions definitely belong to the Islamic religion, and which of them, in fact, were but Arabic, Persian, or Turkish traditions.

Thus, Islamic education must recognize the function of national and modern education, but must not leave them to take over its own function. In the meantime, Islamic education has to distinguish the genuine beliefs and traditions of Islam from the traditions and additions (innovations, *bid'at*) borrowed, first from the Arabs and later from other peoples.

— Reading No. 13 —

THE NINETEENTH-CENTURY REFORMS

Since the seventeenth century the Ottoman leaders had considered reforms in an attempt to save the empire. But not until the ascendancy of Selim III (1789-1807) was the notion that the empire should be modernized along Western lines adopted in earnest. The sultan's efforts were unsuccessful. His successor, Mahmud II (1808-1839), abolished the Janissary Corps and introduced reforms which paved the way for a more systematic transformation of the empire. This came under Abdul Medjid (1839-1861), who with the issuance of the Hatt-i Sherif of Gülhané (November 3, 1839) and the Hatt-i Humayun project of reforms (February 18, 1856) inaugurated the period of the Tanzimat (Regulations), during which far-reaching reforms were introduced.

Hatt-i Sherif of Gülhane,* November 3, 1839

All the world knows that in the first days of the Ottoman Monarchy, the glorious precepts of the Koran and the Laws of the Empire were always honoured. The Empire in consequence increased in strength and greatness, and all her Subjects, without exception, had risen in the highest degree to ease and prosperity. In the last 150 years a succession of accidents and divers causes have arisen which have brought about a disregard for the sacred code of Laws, and the Regulations flowing therefrom, and the former strength and prosperity have changed into weakness and poverty; an Empire in fact loses all its stability so soon as it ceases to observe its Laws.

These considerations are ever present to our mind, and, ever since the day of our advent to the Throne, the thought of the public weal, of the improvement of the state of the Provinces, and of relief to the peoples, has not ceased to engage it. If, therefore, the geographical position of the Ottoman Provinces, the fertility of the soil, the aptitude and intelligence of the inhabitants are considered, the conviction will remain that, by striving to find efficacious means, the result, which by the help of God we hope to attain, can be obtained within a few years. Full of confidence, therefore, in the help of the Most High, assisted by the intercession of our Prophet, we deem it right to seek by new institutions to give to the Provinces composing the Ottoman Empire the benefit of a good Administration.

These institutions must be principally carried out under three heads, which are: 1. The guarantees insuring to our subjects perfect security for life, honour, and fortune. 2. A regular system of assessing and levying Taxes. 3. An equally regular system for the levy of Troops and the duration of their service. . . .

From henceforth, therefore, the cause of every accused person shall be publicly judged in accordance with our Divine Law, after enquiry and examination, and so long as a regular judgment shall not have been pronounced, no one can, secretly or publicly, put another to death by poison or in any other manner.

No one shall be allowed to attack the honour of any other person whatever.

* E. Hertslet, *The Map of Europe by Treaty,* 4 vols. (London: Butterworths, 1875-1891), Vol. II, pp. 1002-1005.

Each one shall possess his Property of every kind, and shall dispose of it in all freedom, without let or hindrance from any person whatever; thus, for example, the innocent Heirs of a Criminal shall not be deprived of their legal rights, and the Property of the Criminal shall not be confiscated.

These Imperial concessions shall extend to all our subjects, of whatever Religion or sect they may be; they shall enjoy them without exceptions. We therefore grant perfect security to the inhabitants of our Empire, in their lives, their honour, and their fortunes, as they are secured to them by the sacred text of our Law. . . .

As all the Public Servants of the Empire receive a suitable salary, and that the salaries of those whose duties have not, up to the present time, been sufficiently remunerated, are to be fixed, a rigorous Law shall be passed against the traffic of favouritism and of appointments (*richvet*), which the Divine Law reprobates, and which is one of the principal causes of the decay of the Empire.

Hatt-i Humayoun,* February 18, 1856

Let it be done as herein set forth.

To you, my Grand Vizier, Mehemed Emin Ali Pasha, decorated with my Imperial Order of the Medjidiyé of the first class, and with the Order of Personal Merit; may God grant to you greatness, and increase your power! . . .

It being now my desire to renew and enlarge still more the new Institutions ordained with the view of establishing a state of things conformable with the dignity of my Empire and— . . . by the kind and friendly assistance of the Great Powers, my noble Allies, . . . The guarantees promised on our part by the Hatti-Humaïoun of Gülhané, and in conformity with the Tanzimat, . . . are today confirmed and consolidated, and efficacious measures shall be taken in order that they may have their full and entire effect.

All the Privileges and Spiritual Immunities granted by my ancestors *ab antiquo,* and at subsequent dates, to all Christian communities or other non-Mussulman persuasions established in my Empire under my protection, shall be confirmed and maintained.

Every Christian or other non-Mussulman community shall be bound within a fixed period, and with the concurrence of a Commission composed *ad hoc* of members of its own body, to proceed with my high approbation and under the inspection of my Sublime Porte, to examine into its actual

* Hertslet, *op. cit.,* Vol. II, pp. 1243-1249.

Immunities and Privileges, and to discuss and submit to my
Sublime Porte the Reforms required by the progress of
civilization and of the age. The powers conceded to the
Christian Patriarchs and Bishops by the Sultan Mahomet
II and his successors, shall be made to harmonize with the
new position which my generous and beneficent intentions
insure to these communities. . . . The principles of nomi-
nating the Patriarchs for life, after the revision of the rules
of election now in force, shall be exactly carried out, con-
formably to the tenor of the Firmans of Investiture. . . .
The ecclesiastical dues, of whatever sort or nature they be,
shall be abolished and replaced by fixed revenues of the
Patriarchs and heads of communities. . . . In the towns,
small boroughs, and villages, where the whole population is
of the same Religion, no obstacle shall be offered to the
repair, according to their original plan, of buildings set apart
for Religious Worship, for Schools, for Hospitals, and for
Cemeteries. . . .

Every distinction or designation tending to make any class
whatever of the subjects of my Empire inferior to another
class, on account of their Religion, Language, or Race, shall
be for ever effaced from the Administrative Protocol. The
laws shall be put in force against the use of any injurious or
offensive term, either among private individuals or on the
part of the authorities.

As all forms of Religion are and shall be freely professed
in my dominions, no subject of my Empire shall be hindered
in the exercise of the Religion that he professes. . . . No
one shall be compelled to change their Religion . . . and
. . . all the subjects of my Empire, without distinction of
nationality, shall be admissible to public employments. . . .
All the subjects of my Empire, without distinction, shall be
received into the Civil and Military Schools of the Government. . . . Moreover, every community is authorized to establish Public Schools of Science, Art, and Industry. . . .

All Commercial, Correctional, and Criminal Suits between
Mussulmans and Christian or other non-Mussulman subjects,
or between Christians or other non-Mussulmans of different
sects, shall be referred to Mixed Tribunals. The proceedings
of these Tribunals shall be public: the parties shall be con-
fronted, and shall produce their witnesses, whose testimony
shall be received, without distinction, upon oath taken according to the religious law of each sect. . . .

Penal, Correctional, and Commercial Laws, and Rules of
Procedure for the Mixed Tribunals, shall be drawn up as soon
as possible, and formed into a code. . . . Proceedings shall
be taken, for the reform of the Penitentiary System. . . .

The organization of the Police . . . shall be revised in such a manner as to give to all the peaceable subjects of my Empire the strongest guarantees for the safety both of their persons and property. . . . Christian subjects, and those of other non-Mussulman sects, . . . shall, as well as Mussulmans, be subject to the obligations of the Law of Recruitment. The principle of obtaining substitutes, or of purchasing exemption, shall be admitted.

Proceedings shall be taken for a Reform in the Constitution of the Provincial and Communal Councils, in order to ensure fairness in the choice of the Deputies of the Mussulman, Christian, and other communities, and freedom of voting in the Councils. . . .

As the Laws regulating the purchase, sale, and disposal of Real Property are common to all the subjects of my Empire, it shall be lawful for Foreigners to possess Landed Property in my dominions. . . .

The Taxes are to be levied under the same denomination from all the subjects of my Empire, without distinction of class or of Religion. The most prompt and energetic means for remedying the abuses in collecting the Taxes, and especially the Tithes, shall be considered. The system of direct collection shall gradually, and as soon as possible, be substituted for the plan of Farming, in all the branches of the Revenues of the State.

A special Law having been already passed, which declared that the Budget of the Revenue and Expenditure of the State shall be drawn up and made known every year, the said law shall be most scrupulously observed. . . .

The heads of each Community and a Delegate, designated by my Sublime Porte, shall be summoned to take part in the deliberations of the Supreme Council of Justice on all occasions which might interest the generality of the subjects of my Empire. . . .

Steps shall be taken for the formation of Banks and other similar institutions, so as to effect a reform in the monetary and financial system, as well as to create Funds to be employed in augmenting the sources of the material wealth of my Empire.

Steps shall also be taken for the formation of Roads and Canals to increase the facilities of communication and increase the sources of the wealth of the country. Everything that can impede commerce or agriculture shall be abolished. . . .

Such being my wishes and my commands, you, who are my Grand Vizier, will, according to custom, cause this Imperial Firman to be published in my capital and in all parts

of my Empire; and will watch attentively, and take all the
necessary measures that all the orders which it contains be
henceforth carried out with the most rigorous punctuality.

— Reading No. 14 —

TURKISM*

*Of all the political philosophers who espoused the cause of
Turkish nationalism none were so distinguished as Ziya
Gökalp, who formulated the theoretical basis of Turkism.
Ziya Gökalp founded in Salonika a review called* Young Pens
*which attracted many young writers and intellectuals. He was
a member of the central committee of the Union and Progress. Critical of the two existing cultures—Ottoman religious
(*ümmet*) culture and Western (*Tanzimat*) culture—Ziya
Gökalp advocated a national (*Turkish*) culture which called
for the Turks to adopt Western civilization while remaining
Turks and Muslims.*

                    ✓   ✓   ✓

Let me put it more clearly: before the rise of Turkism
there were two 'cultures' in our country—the religious
(*ümmet*) 'culture' and the Westernist (*Tanzimat*) 'culture'
—which were inimical to each other. The souls of the educated Turks were torn in the struggle between the two. In
reality, neither reflected the true inner life of the Turks. . . .
It seems, therefore, that when the Turks entered into a
phase of modern and national life, they were sentenced to
remain under the unnatural tutelage of an *ümmet* 'culture,'
which was not modern at all, and of the *Tanzimatist* education, which was not at all national. Both 'cultures' were kept
side by side artificially without any attempt being made to
reconcile and co-ordinate them. The contradictions between
the two were reflected in the souls of young men who had

* Ziya Gökalp, *Turkish Nationalism and Western Civiliza-
      tion,* translated and edited by Niyazi Berkes (New York:
      Columbia University Press, 1959), pp. 285-290, 297.

the psychological aptitude of synthesis and produced crises in their lives. Both 'cultures' were called civilizations. . . .

In reality, however, the two mentalities represented by these two civilizations appeared diametrically opposed to each other only under the influence of certain traditional catchwords and convictions and were not at all irreconcilable. First of all, what had existed then was a national Culture, on the one hand, and two 'culture' patterns in the form of international civilization, on the other. The *ümmet* 'culture' constituted one element of the national Culture in the form of religion. As the Turks were Muslims, Islam would naturally remain in their Culture as an important element. Thus, there would not be a conflict between the *ümmet* 'culture' and the national Culture. Since religion constituted one of the sources of the national Culture, there should be a close solidarity between the two. And, equally, there would be no contradiction between the national Culture and the European 'culture' introduced with the *Tanzimat*. Only those forces which are of the same nature may be contradictory. For example, the Eastern and Western civilizations are absolutely irreconcilable. . . .

Before the Turkist arrived at these conclusions, the false representatives of our culture were the representatives of the *ümmet* and those of the civilization the *Tanzimatists*. Yes, the first were the false representatives of the old 'culture' because insofar as Islam was confined to those highbrows who were educated in Arabic and Persian, it failed to penetrate into the masses. Therefore, with the exception of the religious life, the rest of the *ümmet* 'culture' cannot be called Culture. It is only the religious life within the *ümmet* 'culture' is not reconcilable with Western civilization, the religion of Islam is. . . .

The *Tanzimatists*, on the other hand, were false representatives of contemporary civilization. While European civilization did not aim at destroying the particular Culture of any nation, the *Tanzimatists* entirely neglected the national Culture, equating Culture with civilization which is common to all nations. Their understanding of European civilization did not go beyond that of the Levantines of Pera. They could see Europe only through the eyes of these Levantine *Frenks*. They simply imitated the superficial lustre, the luxury, and ornateness, and such other rubbish of Europe, and never seriously tried to assimilate the science, philosophy, art, and moral standards of its civilization.

We can now argue definitely that a serious interest in Culture is absolutely requisite for the rise of a genuine interest in civilization. For a civilization-group is a society above societies, made up of culture-groups or nations. . . . The nations will cling first to their own ideals; it is only after they have realized the value of a national Culture that a Society of Nations is conceivable. The cosmopolitanism that existed before the era of national idealism is diametrically opposed to present-day internationalism, which is based on international law. In the Europe of today, this old cosmopolitanism no longer exists. Every person is first of all a member of a nation and then of an international community. Among us, as the meaning of nationalism is not understood in its real sense, the fiction of cosmopolitanism is in vogue over against internationalism. . . .

Since truth results from the conflict of ideas, as Namik Kemal said, the conflict between the *ümmet* 'culture' and the *Tanzimat* 'culture' would inevitably give rise to a new sparkle of truth in the souls of the youth who were capable of yearning for a synthesis. The long-awaited sparkle was Turkism with its substitution of the national Culture for *ümmet* 'culture' and of modern civilization for the *Tanzimatist* 'culture.' Turkism is nothing but the method of right feeling and right thinking for the Turks. Right feeling means the avoidance of error in our value judgments; right thinking means the exactness in our judgments on reality. Religious, moral, and aesthetic judgments require right feeling; science, industry, and techniques are based on exact thinking. Since subjective feelings are national and objective ideas international, right feeling means sharing the feelings of the nation and correct thinking means reasoning as all civilized human beings do, on the basis of scientific thought. . . .

We see, therefore, that Turkism first started as a philosophical movement under the name of New Life, and then evolved into a practical movement inevitably arriving at conclusions that are corroborated by present-day sociology. This common conclusion teaches us that human Culture is nothing but a synthesis of national Culture and international civilization and that humanity is heading towards an international society by the federation of free nations.

. . . Once we understand these relations between culture and civilization, we can determine the meaning of Turkism and what it is expected to do. The Ottoman civilization was destined to fall for two reasons: first of all, like all other empires, it was a non-permanent community of peoples. Not communities but societies are groups which have everlasting life; only nations are societies. Subjugated nations may forget their national identity only temporarily under the cosmopolitan rule of the empires. They are destined to awaken from their slumber of serfdom and demand their cultural independence and political sovereignty. This process started in Europe five centuries ago. It was inevitable for those empires —the Austrian, Russian, and Ottoman empires which, so far, had remained safe from this process—to undergo dissolution like their predecessors.

The second reason is the fact that the more Western civilization advanced, the more it increased its power to wipe out the civilization of the East. In Russia and among the Balkan nations the civilization of the West took the place of that of the East [*which is not an Islamic civilization but a continuation of the Byzantine*], and sooner or later the same transformation would take place within the Ottoman territories. . . . As the civilization of the West is taking the place of that of the East everywhere, quite naturally the Ottoman civilization which was a part of Eastern civilization would fall and leave its place to Turkish culture with the religion of Islam, on the one hand, and to Western civilization, on the other. Now, the mission of the Turkists is nothing but to uncover the Turkish culture which has remained in the people, on the one hand, and to graft Western civilization in its entirety and with all its living forms on to the national culture, on the other.

What the reformists of the *Tanzimat* era did was a mere attempt to reconcile the civilizations of East and West. But two opposite civilizations cannot live side by side. As their principles are opposed to each other, each tends to corrupt the other. The principles of Western and Eastern music are irreconcilable. The experimental mind of the West cannot get along with the scholastic mind of the East. A nation is either Eastern or Western. Just as there can be no person with two faiths, so there can be no nation with two civilizations. As the reformists of the *Tanzimat* era failed to see this, they failed in their reforms. The Turkists will succeed, because they have determined to adopt Western civilization as a whole and to drop the originally Byzantine civilization of the East. The Turkists are those who aim at Western civilization while remaining Turks and Muslims. Before they realize this, they have to discover and revive our national culture. . . .

PAN-TURANISM AND PAN-ISLAMISM*

The greatest Turkish woman writer was Halidé Edib. In her many published works and speeches she expressed the spirit and content of the new Turkish nationalism—rooted in the cultural and regional unity of the Ottoman Turks— much of which became the embodiment of the political program of Kemalist Turkey. But she was not completely satisfied with the political course that Kemalist Turkey took, and for a time she and her husband lived abroad. Here she tells us why Pan-Turanism and Pan-Islamism could not work.

✓   ✓   ✓

Pan-Turanism was a larger understanding and definition of the nationalism expressed by Keuk-Alp Zia and some well known writers from the Russian Turks, such as Ahmed Aga-yeff and Youssouf Ackchoura Beys. At first it was purely cultural, but it was developed into a political ideal by some leaders of the Unionist party, especially when the Turkish arms passed into old Russia during the World War. But politically speaking Pan-Turanism never had a clear boundary or a crystallized expression or an explanation. . . . Was it the political unity of all the Turanian people? Had the Christian Turks any place in the Pan-Turanism expressed by the Ottoman Turks? Or was it only meant for the Moslem Turks, which would be some form of the Pan-Islamism of Enver Pasha, who would add racial unity to the religious unity he vaguely imagined to bring forth, and failed.

I differed from Keuk-Alp Zia in his political conception for uniting the Turks. I believed and believe that nationalism is cultural and regional in Turkey, and that it would not be possible to unite the Turks in Russia to us politically in the way we then thought was possible. They themselves follow distinct and national lines, and differ from us very much. Besides they would object to being interfered with by the Ottoman Turks, however much they may admire our litera-

* Halidé Edib Adivar, *Memoirs of Halidé Edib* (New York: The Century Co., n.d.), pp. 312-328.

ture. The elements and influences which are building their culture are distinctly Russian, while those of the Ottoman Turk are distinctly Western. The utmost possible and perhaps the most desirable political connection in the far future, between the Turks up to the Caspian Sea and the Ottoman Turks, would be that of federal states, giving a large and free margin to both elements to realize their individual culture and progress. . . .

Keuk-Alp Zia was really one of the great thinkers of the Unionist regime. Although it is difficult to say who really effected the passage of Pan-Turanism to a political ideal, whether it was Zia himself or the leading politicians of his party, it is clear that Zia at first began it as a purely cultural ideal. He was trying to create a new Turkish mythology which would bridge the abyss between the Ottoman Turks and their Turanism ancestors. He wrote a great many charming stories and poems for children; he tried to popularize his knowledge of the origin of the Turk, and the new ideal of life which he was trying to bring into being. In some of his first works he used words which were archaeologically Turkish, but which sounded dead and artificial. He soon realized his mistake, and in his last works he uses the popular Turkish of his country. . . . He believed that Islamism, as founded by the Arabs, could not suit us, and that if we would not go back to our pagan state we must start a religious reformation more in keeping with our own temperament. He was a warm admirer of the Protestant Reformation, which perhaps truly began the nationalization of the European peoples. He published the "Islamic Review" in which he gave rather a good translation of the Koran in Turkish. In his ideas of religious reform he was greatly influenced by Moussa Bikieff, the Tartar Moslem religious reformer in Kazan. . . .

He was very much under the influence of German philosophy especially under Durkheim. But his last oracle was Bergson. He was, however, very consistent in one point, and that was about the direction of Turkish progress. He believed that the Turk must be Westernized at any cost. Among the many definitions which he tried to give the Turks, the best is his last one: "I am of the Turkish race, Moslem religion, Western civilization." His book called "Turkization, Islamization, Westernization," contains his philosophical and sociological ideas.

Parallel to Keuk-Alp Zia's Pan-Turanism was the Pan-Islamic ideal of Enver Pasha and his followers. If in the late years of the World War they seemed Pan-Turanistic it was because the Turanians whom they thought of uniting with

Turkey were Moslems. But the ideal had as little influence as Pan-Turanism, politically speaking. The separatist tendencies of the Moslem units such as the Arabs and the Albanians discredited Pan-Islamism. Besides, the young and the reforming elements feared it as an element of reaction and fanaticism. An intelligent understanding of the aspirations and the needs of the Moslem minorities might have helped to justify Enver Pasha's Pan-Islamism. As it was, only the Moslems outside of Turkey showed any interest at all. The fear of the Allies about Pan-Islamism was quite groundless, and their attribution of all movements of self-assertion among their own Moslem subjects to Turkish influence was and, above all, is groundless.

Nationalism found its first external organization in Turk Yourdu, a kind of literary and cultural club formed by the Turkish students in Geneva in 1910. As it had some fine students from among the Russian Turks, its spirit was Pan-Turanistic, at least culturally. It issued non-periodical reviews and continues to do so, some of which contain unusually fine literature and studies on Turkology. . . .

The capital soon followed the example. The founding of Turk Yourdu in Istanboul was chiefly and primarily one of the many intellectual undertakings of the Union and Progress. . . . The organization published a weekly which goes on to this day. It was edited by Youssouf Akchura, who was openly and decidedly anti-Unionist, although an avowed and sincere Pan-Turanist. He made a great success of the paper, and it had perhaps more readers among the Turks in Russia than in Turkey. Akchura, a believer in the superiority of the Russian Turk to the Ottoman Turk, advocated warmly the necessary cultural unity of the Turks. . . .

The external expression of nationalism went one degree deeper and propagated itself among the younger generation, especially the students. The medical faculty has the historical honor of starting almost every new movement, especially when it is directed against personal tyranny of despots and regimes, or the tyranny of reaction and ignorance. It had given the greatest number of victims to Abdul Hamid's tyranny. But it would be interesting to note in this instance how and why the Turkish student has thought of himself as something separate and different from the other Ottoman students of the empire. . . .

After 1908 all the non-Turkish elements in Turkey, Christian and Moslem, had political and national clubs. When the Turkish students of the universities saw their fellow-students, whom they had so far identified with themselves, belonging

to separate organizations, with national names and separate
interests, they began to wonder. . . .

. . . For the first time reduced to his elements and torn
from the ensemble of races in Turkey, he vaguely faced the
possibility of searching, analyzing, and discovering himself as
something different from the rest. . . .

The first separate organization formed by the Turkish
youth in this sense was called the Turk Ojak (Turkish
Hearth). So it was in 1911 that the first national club was
founded. The founders were a few medical students who kept
their names secret. The fundamental spirit of equality and
fraternity of the Ojak was an established tradition then. . . .

Two dominant clauses which were never allowed to be
altered by the general congress, and which show the tendencies and the spirit of the Ojak are: first, the Ojak will help
the cultural development of the Turk; second, the Ojak is not
a political institution. . . .

The most active period of the Ojak began when Hamdullah
Soubhi Bey became the president. . . . Besides the majority
of young students, the majority of Turkish writers and leading men also belonged to it, and worked with admirable
idealism for the cultural development of the Turk. Lectures
and free lessons were opened to the public by well known
men, among whom Keuk-Alp Zia was the most prominent.
Men belonging to all shades of political creeds and ideals
gathered in sincere understanding under its roof.

The clubs helped the Turkish students from all over the
Turkish world to obtain their education in Istanbul. The
Ojak, which showed Pan-Turanistic tendencies culturally, was
against Pan-Islamism, but in a few years Pan-Turanism also
gave way to a regional nationalism which can be defined as
belonging to Turkey proper and the peoples who live in
it. . . .

As nationalism is considered a narrow ideal by those who
aim at the welfare of humanity and hope to obtain it through
internationalism, I have often been reproached by my international friends. And as I have not ceased to work for the
happiness of my kind, especially of those who are nearest
to me, I have honestly tried to analyze the inner meaning
of my nationalism, whether it can hurt others who are not
Turks, whether it can hurt in the long run the family of
nations in the world to which Turkey also belongs.

The individual or the nation, in order to understand its
fellow-men or its fellow-nations, in order to create beauty
and to express its personality, must go deep down to the roots
of its being and study itself sincerely. The process of this

deep self-duty, as well as its results, is nationalism. I believe with all earnestness that such a national self-study, and the exchange of its results, is the first and right step to international understanding and love of the peoples and nations.

— Reading No. 16 —

TURKISH-AMERICAN RELATIONS*

It was not until 1799 that the young American republic took first formal steps toward the establishment of diplomatic relations with Turkey. The interference of foreign powers, particularly England, the unfavorable international situation, difficulties in dealing with the Porte, and the absence of urgency, contributed to the delay in the conclusions of a treaty until May 10, 1830. The legation was opened in the following year and from then on the economic and diplomatic intercourse between the two countries steadily expanded, though not without problems.

✓   ✓   ✓

In 1774 when John Adams, Benjamin Franklin, and Thomas Jefferson were appointed treaty Commissioners the Continental Congress included the Ottoman Empire in the list of countries with which they might negotiate. In those days Turkey was much more populous than the United States and, before the Louisiana purchase, much larger. . . .

The Minister's [*Rufus King, Minister to England*] reports led President Adams on February 8, 1799, to nominate William Smith of Charleston, South Carolina, who was then Minister to Portugal, as Envoy Extraordinary and Minister Plenipotentiary to the Sublime Porte with full powers to negotiate a treaty. But the newly appointed Minister, although he accepted the mission, never received instructions and never reached Constantinople. International complications arising

* Leland James Gordon, *American Relations With Turkey* (Philadelphia: University of Pennsylvania Press, 1932), pp. 8-12.

out of the Franco-British War were chiefly responsible for abandonment of the mission. Great Britain and Russia were allies of Turkey in the campaign to drive Napoleon out of Egypt. Sentiment in America being strongly pro-French, it was argued that to negotiate a treaty with Turkey at that time would strain Franco-American relations.

Continuance of international complications resulted in the postponement of negotiations until 1820. In that year Luther Bradish went to Constantinople for the purpose of reporting on the possibility and desirability of negotiating a treaty. On December 20, 1820, he reported that the negotiation of a treaty would be desirable from a commercial standpoint since American traders were compelled to pay a 5 per cent duty, whereas the merchants of other nations paid only 3 per cent. The estimated cost of negotiating a treaty was placed at $50,000. He recommended the postponement of negotiations, however, owing to the political situation in Turkey arising out of the Greek revolution, and the Porte's desire to conciliate England, whose opposition to a Turco-American accord had previously been revealed.

Mr. George P. English, who was asked to investigate the possibility of successfully concluding negotiations in 1823, reported that the opposition and intrigues of European powers had prevented all previous attempts to approach the Sublime Porte. In order to meet the situation he recommended secret negotiations between the Commander of the Mediterranean Squadron and Capudan Paşa.

Following that suggestion Commodore John Rodgers was authorized in 1825 to negotiate secretly with the Turkish official. His instructions were to secure the right to trade with all Turkish ports; to be allowed to appoint Consuls at such ports as American interests might require; and to secure freedom of movement through the Dardanelles. The Capudan Paşa wrote on February 7, 1828, that the Sublime Porte was then prepared to negotiate.

Six months later President Adams appointed Captain William Crane, a naval officer, and David Offley, as Commissioners to negotiate a treaty. An appropriation of $20,000 was provided to carry on the negotiations. . . .

The Crane-Offley mission was unsuccessful in concluding negotiations, for the attempt to levy higher duties on American merchandise than those paid by other powers was stoutly resisted, as was the Turkish demand to have certain ships constructed in America with the implication that they should be presented as gifts in exchange for the treaty.

On September 12, 1829, President Andrew Jackson appointed Captain James Biddle, David Offley, and Charles

Rhind, one of the oldest American merchants trading in the Levant, as Commissioners to negotiate a treaty. In his instructions to those Commissioners Secretary of State Martin Van Buren informed them that "the trade between the United States and the Turkish dominion, though very limited in its range, and without the security derived from treaty stipulations, is, even under such adverse circumstances, very considerable." He also informed them of previous intrigues on the part of European powers which had successfully prevented the conclusion of a treaty and instructed them to report any such interference. . . .

Previous negotiations had ceased when Mr. Offley had refused to accede to the stipulation that goods coming from the United States should pay 5 per cent, whereas merchandise originating in European countries was admitted after payment of a 3 per cent duty. A proposed compromise had cut the difference to one-half per cent but Mr. Offley had been determined in his stand for complete equality.

Negotiations were opened on February 8, 1830, resulting in the signature of a treaty on May 10 by Mr. Rhind who signed alone, a rift having developed among the Commissioners. In order to please the Sultan and make it appear that something had been given in return for his concessions on the matter of equality of duties with other powers a secret article was included in the treaty. It provided the privilege of consulting the American Minister to be appointed as to the best method of making a contract to procure ships and ships' timber. The article was innocuous, however, for it was agreed that it need not be signed and the Senate promptly rejected it. But the treaty itself was accepted and marked the beginning of formal relations between the United States and the Ottoman Empire one hundred years ago. . . .

There was some feeling on the part of the Sublime Porte that the United States did not properly esteem the new diplomatic post, for Commodore Porter who was sent to exchange ratifications and to remain as the representative of his Government was only given the rank of *Chargé d'Affaires,* whereas the Porte maintained that at least a Minister Plenipotentiary should have been assigned. Considerable stir also was caused over the matter of presents, so vital to the negotiation of an Oriental treaty in those days. When the presents were sent to the Sublime Porte Commodore Porter marked on each one its value in order that there might be no doubt that his Government had not failed properly to reward the Turkish officials. Upon receipt of the gifts the Reis Effendi wrote a polite note to the Commodore telling him that if he had paid as much for his presents as the notation indicated he had paid far too much. The American representative suspected that an attempt was being made to belittle the gifts and to secure still more. . . .

An appropriation of $36,500 having been approved, an American Legation was opened in Constantinople March 2, 1831. With the exception of the years 1917 to 1919 the Legation, which was raised to the rank of Embassy in 1906, has continuously represented the interests of the United States in Turkey, but one hundred years later the Treaty itself had passed into the realm of history, being replaced by the Treaty of Ankara signed October 1, 1929, and proclaimed April 21, 1930.

— Reading No. 17 —

AMERICAN MISSIONARIES IN TURKEY*

The American missionaries arrived in Turkey in the 1840's. After 1864 they encountered serious obstacles in their work. According to strict interpretation of Islamic law the penalty for a change of faith is death. Consequently the Christian missionaries had difficulty in reaching the Muslims, who were forbidden to attend Christian schools. The only important contacts that the missionaries had with them came through medical services and at private meetings. The medical missionaries from America rendered a very valuable service in Turkey. The first medical missionary was Dr. Azariah Smith. The centenary of a hospital founded in his name at Gaziantep was celebrated in 1947. The missionaries likewise did great work in the field of education. The largest American colleges—Robert College for men and the American College for girls—were sustained by the Near East College Association in New York. For the first fifty years after it was opened in 1863 Robert College taught only Christian boys; Muslim children were not permitted to en-

* Leland James Gordon, *American Relations With Turkey* (Philadelphia: University of Pennsylvania Press, 1932), pp. 232-36.

roll. The same is true of the American College, founded in 1871 as a high school and raised to the level of college in 1890.

✓ ✓ ✓

Not only was there a conscious policy of opposition, but the nature of the Ottoman Government was such as to increase the difficulties of American missionaries as the extension of their work took them far into the interior. . . . There was little security of life and property in certain of those provinces and there was no satisfaction in protesting to the Sublime Porte for it was powerless to take action against the provincial officials even if it so desired. As late as 1895 an American naval officer who had been sent to protect his fellow citizens in Turkey expressed the opinion that "the governor of Massachusetts is as much liable for the murder of settlers by the Apaches as is the governor of Smyrna for the murder of Armenians by the Koords."

During the first years of the Ottoman reaction against missions the United States Government was ineffective in protecting the rights of its citizens. There are a number of explanations for that situation. The American interpretation of exterritorial rights as granted by the Treaty of 1830 was denied by the Sublime Porte. American preoccupation with the Civil War and the following period of reconstruction demanded first attention. Although the Ottoman Government was a supporter of the Union cause during the Civil War, it was believed in American governmental circles that the internal struggle being waged injured what little prestige the American Government had built up in Turkey. Moreover, that period in history marked the height of secret diplomacy in international affairs. Officials of the Sublime Porte, long accustomed to maintaining their empire through playing one power against another, did not respond to the American policy of open diplomacy. In no other part of the world was prestige more important and in no other region had the people been so continuously governed by force. In 1892 Secretary of State Foster wrote to Minister Thompson that "it appears to be a characteristic of Turkish policy to seek to limit foreign rights and privileges in detail, and to wear away, by the slow process of erosion, what it may not overcome by power." Under those circumstances the governments which were ready and willing to resort to the use of force or to a threat of force enjoyed the highest prestige in Constantinople. It was well known that when the foreign offices of London, Paris or Berlin protested an action by the Sublime Porte that men of war stood ready to occupy some strategic portion of the Empire. Consequently, protests by those powers usually resulted in effective guarantees. On the other hand, the presence of American naval vessels was a rare and uncommon sight in the harbor of Constantinople and the belief on the part of Ottoman authorities that the United States Government would not resort to force played no small part in the early difficulties experienced in securing recognition of treaty rights for its nationals.

In addition to the factors mentioned, it was asserted that there was a total lack of interest in missions and schools on the part of American Ministers in the period from 1860 to 1880. . . .

Robert College was not the only American institution suffering from lack of adequate governmental support. By 1885 the situation had become so serious that the Secretary of the American Board addressed a formal complaint to the President of the United States calling attention "to the need of more efficient protection of American interests in the Turkish Empire." The protest registered four general complaints involving restrictions on the sale of religious literature, on the issuance of building permits for schools, the exemption of missionary imports from payment of customs duties and the insecurity of American missionaries in their lives and property. . . .

As Ottoman opposition increased in the late nineteenth century and the number of American complaints grew, there was a noticeable change beginning about 1890 in the attitude of the United States Government. The official representatives of the United States displayed a new attitude and adopted aggressive methods in protecting the rights of all Americans in Turkey. The use of naval vessels was frequently resorted to and in some cases there was a virtual display of force. The dispatches to the Sublime Porte became more commanding and peremptory in nature, with frequent threats to resort to extreme action if satisfaction were not obtained. The new policy yielded immediate results. In December, 1896, in answer to an inquiry addressed to him by Minister Terrell, Rev. H. O. Dwight reported that he knew of no case of violence inflicted by the Turkish Government or by Ottoman subjects on the missionaries of the American Board since March, 1893. No schools had been closed and instruction had not ceased for any cause in any mission school since the massacres began in 1893.

In view of the distressing events which marked the last ten years of the nineteenth century and of the continued disturbances in the first ten years of the twentieth century,

it may be asserted that if the Government of the United
States had not adopted a vigorous policy the work of American missionaries and educational institutions might have
been reduced to negligible proportions.

The present policy of the United States Government was
well summarized by Secretary Hughes in 1922 when he
reiterated the policy that American missions must receive the
full support of the government.

While the United States governmental policy has grown
more firm, Turkish policy has grown still more antagonistic
toward the strictly religious aspect of missionary activity. As
a result of the Turkish attitude and of the loss of capitula-
tory privileges the position of foreign missions in Turkey
today is more precarious than ever before. In 1887 the government had the disposition to bring disaster on the missions but
lacked the power and courage. Today the government has
the power and courage to stop all mission work, but as long
as missions adhere to rules it lacks the disposition.

— Reading No. 18 —

GERMAN PENETRATION OF TURKEY*

*In the 1830's the Turks for the first time hired Germans
(among them Helmuth von Moltke) to train their army.
Again in the 1880's they did this on a more ambitious scale.
The extension of German influence over the Turkish military
establishment coincided with the gradual German political
and economic ascendancy in Istanbul after 1878. German
investments in industry and railway construction mounted.
The projected Berlin-Baghdad Railway line, to be built by
Germans, alarmed the European powers and aggravated the
international situation. With the invitation of General Liman
von Sanders' mission for the reorganization of the army on
the eve of the First World War, Germany established a firm
position in Turkey.*

* Djemal Pasha, *Memories of a Turkish Statesman—1913-
    1919* (London: Hutchinson & Co. Ltd., 1922), pp. 66-
    68. Reprinted by permission of the publishers.

Last but not least he [*Mahmud Shefket Pasha*] took up the question of the re-organization of the army and navy. A British Naval Mission was already at work. He got into personal touch with the head of that Mission and asked him to accelerate the reorganization of the Navy. As regards the organization of the Army I will now relate the facts, the details of which were given to me by Mahmud Shefket Pasha personally, so that their accuracy cannot be doubted.

During the Pasha's term of office as Grand Vizier he usually spent the night and slept at the Sublime Porte, and as I slept at the Military Governor's Headquarters he called me to the telephone after dinner on several evenings when he felt very tired after heavy work during the day and asked me to go round and see him. On these occasions he often told me of his ideas and plans and asked my opinion.

On one of these evenings he remarked:

"I believe that everything we have done hitherto with regard to the reorganisation of our army has been only half measures, if not bad measures. All the organisers whom we have had here, both during the reign of Sultan Abdul Hamid and since the promulgation of the constitution, have been selected quite casually, and on no definite principle. We have never thought of inviting a serious mission with an adequate and well-thought-out programme and personnel, whose selection must be determined exclusively with reference to that programme.

"Look at the Greeks, for example. They were much cleverer than ourselves. They have entrusted the reorganisation of their navy to the English, and that of their army to the French. . . .

"In my view the greatest service Venizelos has rendered his country was in organising the armed forces of the nation. . . .

"As regards our army, I don't think we must hesitate any longer to adopt the methods of the Germans. For more than thirty years we have had German instructors in our army, our Corps of Officers is trained entirely on German lines, and our army is absolutely familiar with the spirit of German training and military education. It is quite impossible to change all that now. I therefore intend to send for a German military mission on the grand scale and, if necessary, I shall even appoint a German general to command a Turkish army corps, place German staff and regimental officers in command of every unit comprising it, and in this way form a model army corps. The staff and regimental officers of the other corps would have to be posted to this corps for a definite period in order to expand and complete their training. I will also have this mission accompanied by many specialists whose task it will be to reorganise the various departments of the War Office, the General Staff and the military schools and factories. I think that we shall have no occasion for a war for a long time, and I will therefore reduce the *cadres* as much as possible and restore the peace establishment, so that we can effect economies which will enable me to meet the expenses of the reorganization mission. I will give the Turkish world an army which will certainly be small but, on the other hand, well organised and trained. In time of war it will not be difficult to bring this army up to maximum strength by expanding the *cadres*. I am now inquiring of the Germans on what terms they would be prepared to send us some such mission, and consider it advisable to leave the question of their conditions entirely to them."

Such are the circumstances under which General Liman von Sanders' mission for the reorganisation of our army was invited to Constantinople. Enver Pasha had nothing to do with this affair and played no part whatever in it.

After Mahmud Shefket Pasha's death his successor at the War Office, Izzet Pasha, had the same idea, and took up the same line as his predecessor. During his period of office an agreement with reference to the mission was drawn up and concluded. On the day of the arrival in Constantinople of Liman von Sanders and his officers they were met at the station by Izzet Pasha and, in fact, it was a month or six weeks after the arrival of the mission that Enver Pasha became War Minister.

It was Enver Pasha who first pointed out the obstacles to be overcome if the command of the First Army Corps was to be entrusted to Liman von Sanders Pasha. He thought that it would be better to employ the head of the mission in the capacity of an Inspector-General rather than give him the command of an army corps. It was wholly and solely as a result of his suggestion, not under pressure from the Russians, French and English that this change was made.

MUSTAFA KEMAL (ATATÜRK) ON PAST AND FUTURE*

How Mustafa Kemal emerged from obscurity to fame is one of the most fascinating chapters in modern history of Turkey. We know that he was early disillusioned in the Ottoman Empire which he considered a ramshackle structure impossible to preserve. He rejected Ottomanism, Pan-Islamism, and Pan-Turkism and stood for the relinquishment of the empire and the foundation of a homogeneous national Turkish state. In the following quotations we find the essential elements of his political philosophy.

✓   ✓   ✓

Gentlemen,

I landed at Samsoon on the 19th of May, 1919. This was the position at that time:

The group of Powers which included the Ottoman Government had been defeated in the Great War. The Ottoman Army had been crushed on every front. An armistice had been signed under severe conditions. The prolongation of the Great War had left the people exhausted and empoverished. Those who had driven the people and the country into the general conflict had fled and now cared for nothing but their own safety. Wahideddin, the degenerate occupant of the throne and the Caliphate, was seeking for some despicable way to save his person and his throne, the only objects of his anxiety. The Cabinet, of which Damad Ferid Pasha was the head, was weak and lacked dignity and courage. It was subservient to the will of the Sultan alone and agreed to every proposal that could protect its members and their sovereign.

The Army had been deprived of their arms and ammunition, and this state of affairs continued.

* *A Speech delivered by Ghazi Mustapha Kemal, President of the Turkish Republic, October 1927* (Leipzig: K. F. Koehler, Publisher, 1929), pp. 9, 376-379, 393, 480-481, 567, 580-581.

The Entente Powers did not consider it necessary to respect the terms of the armistice. On various pretexts, their men-of-war and troops remained at Constantinople. The Vilayet of Adana was occupied by the French; Urfah, Marash, Aintab, by the English. In Adalia and Konia were the Italians, whilst at Merifun and Samsoon were English troops. Foreign officers and officials and their special agents were very active in all directions. At last, on the 15th May, that is to say, four days before the following account of events begins, the Greek Army, with the consent of the Entente Powers, had landed at Smyrna. Christian elements were also at work all over the country, either openly or in secret, trying to realise their own particular ambitions and thereby hasten the breakdown of the Empire. . . .

*   *   *

Gentlemen:

. . . Among the Ottoman rulers there were some who endeavoured to form a gigantic empire by seizing Germany and West-Rome. One of these rulers hoped to unite the whole Islamic world in one body, to lead it and govern it. For this purpose he obtained control of Syria and Egypt and assumed the title of Caliph. Another Sultan pursued the twofold aim, on the one hand of gaining the mastery over Europe, and on the other of subjecting the Islamic world to his authority and government. The continuous counter-attacks from the West, the discontent and insurrections in the Mohamedan world, as well as the dissensions between the various elements which this policy had artificially brought together within certain limits, had the ultimate result of burying the Ottoman Empire, in the same way as many others, under the pall of history.

What particularly interests foreign policy and upon which it is founded is the internal organisation of the State. Thus it is necessary that the foreign policy should agree with the internal organisation. In a State which extends from the East to the West and which unites in its embrace contrary elements with opposite characters, goals and culture, it is natural that the internal organisation should be defective and weak in its foundations. In these circumstances its foreign policy, having no solid foundation, cannot be strenuously carried on. In the same proportion as the internal organisation of such a State suffers specially from the defect of not being national, so also its foreign policy must lack this character. For this reason, the policy of the Ottoman State was not national but individual. It was deficient in clarity and continuity.

To unite different nations under one common name, to

give these different elements equal rights, subject them to the same conditions and thus to found a mighty State is a brilliant and attractive political ideal; but it is a misleading one. It is an unrealisable aim to attempt to unite in one tribe the various races existing on the earth, thereby abolishing all boundaries. Herein lies a truth which the centuries that have gone by and the men who have lived during these centuries have clearly shown in dark and sanguinary events.

There is nothing in history to show how the policy of Panislamism could have succeeded or how it could have found a basis for its realisation on this earth. As regards the result of the ambition to organise a State which should be governed by the idea of world-supremacy and include the whole of humanity without distinction of race, history does not afford examples of this. For us, there can be no question of the lust of conquest. On the other hand, the theory which aims at founding a "humanitarian" State which shall embrace all mankind in perfect equality and brotherhood and at bringing it to the point of forgetting separatist sentiments and inclinations of every kind, is subject to conditions which are peculiar to itself.

The political system which we regard as clear and fully realisable is national policy. In view of the general conditions obtaining in the world at present and the truths which in the course of centuries have rooted themselves in the minds of and have formed the characters of mankind, no greater mistake could be made than that of being a utopian. This is borne out in history and is the expression of science, reason and common sense.

In order that our nation should be able [to] live a happy, strenuous and permanent life, it is necessary that the State should pursue an exclusively national policy and that this policy should be in perfect agreement with our internal organisation and be based on it. When I speak of national policy, I mean it in this sense: To work within our national boundaries for the real happiness and welfare of the nation and the country by, above all, relying on our own strength in order to retain our existence. But not to lead the people to follow fictitious aims, of whatever nature, which could only bring them misfortune, and expect from the civilised world civilised human treatment, friendship based on mutuality. . . .

*   *   *

Our aim is to secure the complete independence of our nation and the integrity of our territory within its national frontiers. We shall fight and conquer every Power, whichever it might be, who would try to block our way and hinder us from the realisation of this aim. We are absolutely firm in our conviction and our determination. . . .

*   *   *

Thirty-seven days later, on the 25th September, I considered it necessary to make certain explanations to the Assembly at a secret sitting. After I had satisfied the prevailing conceptions, I developed the following ideas:

It is not necessary that the Turkish Nation and the High Assembly should occupy themselves so minutely with the Caliphate and the Monarchy, with the Caliph and the Sultan, while we are struggling to secure the existence and independence of our country. Our higher interests demand that we should not discuss this at all at the present moment. If the question should arise as to whether we ought to remain loyal and true to the present Caliph and Sultan—well, this man is a traitor, he is a tool of the enemy employed against our country and our nation. If the nation considers him in the light of Caliph and Sultan, it will be obliged to obey his orders and thereby realise the enemy's plans and designs. Moreover, a personage who would be a traitor and could be prevented from exercising his authority and making use of the power bestowed upon him by his position, could not hold the exalted title of Caliph or Sultan. If you want to say: 'Let us depose him and choose someone else in his place,' this would lead to no way out of the difficulty, because the present state of affairs and the conditions prevailing at this hour would not allow of it being done. For the person who must be dethroned is not in the midst of his nation but in the hands of the enemy, and if we intended to ignore his existence and recognise someone in his stead, the present Caliph and Sultan would not surrender his rights, but would retain the seat he occupies to-day with his Ministry in Constantinople and would continue to carry on his office. Will the nation and the High Assembly in such an event abandon their high aims and throw themselves into a fight for a Caliph? Shall we then once more witness the times of Ali and Muavija (the fights of the immediate successors of Mohamed)? In short, this question is of far-reaching importance and difficulty. Its solution is not one which we are struggling to discover to-day. . . .

*   *   *

Telegram. Personal.   5th September, 1922
     To the President of the Council of Ministers.
     Reply.

The Greek army has been decisively defeated in Anatolia. Any serious resistance in future will be impossible. There is no reason to enter into any negotiations with regard to the question of Anatolia. The armistice can only be discussed with reference to Thrace. If the Greek Government should appeal to us before the 10th September, directly or through the official mediation of Great Britain, they must be answered by a communication containing the conditions as follow. After this time has elapsed, that is to say after the 10th September, our reply could possibly be formulated differently. In that case I must personally be informed to that effect:

1. Within a fortnight from the date of the armistice, Thrace must be unconditionally restored up to its frontiers of 1914 to the civil and military authorities of the Government of the Grand National Assembly of Turkey.

2. Our prisoners of war in Greece will be transported within a fortnight to the harbours of Smyrna, Panderma and Ismidt.

3. Greece will bind herself forthwith to repair the devastations made by her army during the last three-and-a-half years in Anatolia, as well as those she is still making.

Mustapha Kemal,
Commander-in-Chief,
President of the Grand National Assembly.

*   *   *

I prefer to confront public opinion with actual facts. By these means you will be able to understand in a natural manner into what degrading position a nation possessing pride and a noble heart can be brought by a wretch who, thanks to the fatal succession to the throne, had inherited a noble position and an exalted title.

Indeed, it is sad to think that a creature like Wahideddin, who was low enough to consider that his life and liberty could have been in danger, from whatever cause it might be, in the midst of his own people, had been able to stand even for a single instant at the head of a nation. It is fortunate that the nation has driven this wretch from his hereditary throne and has put an end thereby to the long series of his basenesses. This intervention of the Turkish people is worthy of the highest praise.

An incapable and low creature, without heart or intelligence, might well place himself under the protection of any foreigner who is willing to accept him, but it is surely inappropriate to think that such an individual should bear the title of Caliph of the whole of Islam. To make such an idea understandable, all Mohamedan communities would, first of all, have been reduced to the position of slaves. Is that actually the case in the world?

We Turks are a people who during the whole of our historic existence have been the very embodiment of freedom and independence. Also, we have proved that we are capable of putting an end to the comedy played by the Caliph who exposed himself to humiliations of every description for the miserable object of dragging out an unworthy existence for a few days longer. Acting as we have done, we have confirmed the truth that individuals, and especially those who are base enough to think only of their personal positions and their own lives—even to the injury of the state and nation to which they belong—cannot be of any importance in the mutual relationship of states and nations.

In international relations it must be the ardent wish of the whole civilised world to put an end to the time when the system of puppets governs policy.

BIBLIOGRAPHY

Alderson, A. D., *The Structure of the Ottoman Dynasty* (Oxford, 1956).

Berkes, Niyazi, "Historical Background of Turkish Secularism," in R. N. Frye, ed., *Islam and the West* (The Hague, 1957), pp. 41-68.

Brockelmann, Carl, *History of the Islamic Peoples* (New York, 1947). Tr. by Joel Carlmichael and Moshe Perlmann.

Creasy, Edward S., *History of the Ottoman Turks* (Beirut: Khayats, 1961). Tr. by Zeine N. Zeine.

Davison, Roderic H., *Reform in the Ottoman Empire 1856-1878* (Princeton, 1963).

Devereux, Robert, *The First Ottoman Constitutional Period* (Baltimore, 1963).

Encyclopaedia of Islam, 1st edition, 4 vols. and Supplement (Leiden, 1913-1918), 2nd edition, (Leiden 1954-   ).

Fisher, Sydney Nettleton, *The Middle East* (New York, 1959).

Gibb, E. J. W., *A History of Ottoman Poetry,* 6 vols. (London, 1900-1909).

Gibb, H. A. R., and Harold Bowen, *Islamic Society and the West,* Vol. 1, Part 1 (London, 1950), Part 2 (London, 1957).

Hammer-Purgstall, Joseph von, *Geschichte des osmanischen Reiches* (10-vol. ed., Pest, 1827-1833).

Hitti, Philip, *The Near East in History* (Princeton, 1961).

Hurewitz, H. C., *Diplomacy in the Near and Middle East: A Documentary Record,* 2 vols. (Princeton, 1956).

Iorga, N., *Geschichte des osmanischen Reiches* (5 vols., Gotha, 1908-1913).

Khadduri, M., and H. J. Liebesny, *Land in the Middle East* (Washington, 1955).

Lewis, Bernard, *The Emergence of Modern Turkey* (London, 1961).

Luke, Harry S., *The Making of Modern Turkey from Byzantium to Angora* (London, 1936).

Lybyer, Albert Howe, *The Government of the Ottoman Empire in the Time of Suleiman the Magnificent* (Cambridge, Mass., 1913).

Marriott, J. A. R., *The Eastern Question* (Oxford, 1947).

Mardin, Serif, *The Genesis of Young Ottoman Thought* (Princeton, 1962).

Miller, Barnette, *The Palace School of Muhammad the Conqueror* (Cambridge, Mass., 1941).

Miller, William, *The Ottoman Empire and Its Successors, 1801-1927* (Cambridge, 1936).

Pears, Sir E., *Forty Years in Constantinople* (London, 1916).

Ramsaur, Ernest E., *The Young Turks* (Princeton, 1957).

Robinson, Richard, *The First Turkish Republic* (Cambridge, 1963).

Shaw, Stanford, *The Financial and Administrative Organization and Development of Ottoman Egypt 1517-1798* (Princeton, 1958).

Stavrianos, L. S., *The Balkans Since 1453* (New York, 1958).

Vaughan, Dorothy M., *Europe and the Turk. A Pattern of Alliances 1350-1700* (Liverpool, [1954]).

Wittek, Paul, *The Rise of the Ottoman Empire* (London, 1938).

Zinkeisen, J. W., *Geschichte des osmanischen Reiches in Europa* (7 vols., Hamburg and Gotha, 1840-1863).

INDEX

189